W9-CNR-068

Gay and Lesbian Communities the World Over

Gay and Lesbian Communities the World Over

Rita J. Simon and Alison Brooks

LEXINGTON BOOKS
A division of
ROWMAN & LITTLEFIELD PUBLISHERS, INC.
Lanham • Boulder • New York • Toronto • Plymouth, UK

Published by Lexington Books
A division of Rowman & Littlefield Publishers, Inc.
A wholly owned subsidary of The Rowman & Littlefield Publishing Group, Inc.
4501 Forbes Boulevard, Suite 200, Lanham, Maryland 20706
http://www.lexingtonbooks.com

Estover Road, Plymouth PL6 7PY, United Kingdom

Copyright © 2009 by Lexington Books

British Library Cataloguing in Publication Information Available

Library of Congress Cataloging-in-Publication Data

Simon, Rita J. (Rita James), 1931-
  Gay and lesbian communities the world over / Rita J. Simon and Alison M.
Brooks.
    p. cm.
  ISBN 978-0-7391-4364-3 (cloth : alk. paper) — ISBN 978-0-7391-4366-7
(electronic)
  1. Gays. 2. Lesbians. 3. Homosexuality—History. 4. Homosexuality—
Religious aspects. I. Brooks, Alison, 1985- II. Title.
  HQ76.25.S56 2009
  306.76'6--dc22   2009039586

∞™ The paper used in this publication meets the minimum requirements
of American National Standard for Information Sciences—Permanence of
Paper for Printed Library Materials, ANSI/NISO Z39.48-1992. Printed in the
United States of America

Table of Contents

PART II. REPORTS ON GAYS AND LESBIANS COUNTRY BY COUNTRY

Introduction

In this thirteenth volume in *The World Over* series we examine and compare the rights and statuses of gay and lesbian communities across twenty-one countries. The countries included are Canada, the United States, Argentina, Brazil, Great Britain, France, Germany, Italy, Sweden, Hungary, Poland, Russia, Israel, Egypt, Iran, Nigeria, South Africa, India, China, Japan, and Australia.

From biblical times to the present day, the issue of homosexuality has been addressed by many cultures and countries. In the Bible, from Leviticus we read, "You shall not be with a male as one lies with a female. If there is a man who lies with a male as those who lie with a woman, both of them have committed a detestable act; they shall be put to death." From Deuteronomy: "A woman shall not wear man's clothing, nor shall a man put on woman's clothing." From Romans: Homosexuality is unnaturally indecent; "degrading passion," "insatiable lust."

In ancient Greece, male homosexuality was not seen as "unnatural." It was actually glorified by poets and philosophers and widely accepted by society. In ancient Rome no religious or ethical principle made homosexual acts between men immoral or illegal.

During the Middle Ages, lesbianism was not believed to exist. The Christian fathers claimed that "decent" women do not have sexuality so how can any woman be a lesbian?

As we show in the chapter "Christianity and Homosexuality," some Christian denominations are more accepting than others.

In 1463, the Court of Holland convicted a man of homosexuality (sodomy) and he was burned at the stake. A year later, his partner was whipped down the streets of the Hague and had his hair burned off his head. In Christian Europe, the execution of homosexual men increased from the fifteenth century until ending in the early 1800s. Nearly a thousand sodomy trials were conducted in Holland from 1730 to 1811 and between 1730 and 1932, 75 "sodomites" were sentenced to death. Convicted homosexuals were strangled with a cord either privately in the cellars of city halls or publicly on scaffolds in front of large audiences.

Although the first modern day discussion of homosexuality was not until 1886, communities have dealt with gay and lesbian issues for several centuries preceding that.[1] Discussions of a homosexual "identity" are relatively recent, as well as court cases legalizing sodomy.[2] One famous early case dealing with homosexuality was the 1895 Old Bailey case involving Oscar Wilde. Wilde sued the Marquess of Queensberry for libel after he left Wilde an obscene message at his club accusing him of homosexuality.[3] During the time of the trial, Queensberry's lawyers uncovered evidence of Wilde's association with boy prostitutes and Wilde subsequently dropped the case only to be arrested on charges of "gross indecency" and sentenced to two years hard labor.[4] His story was later adapted into both a book and a film.

In a talk at Columbia University in New York City in March 2008, the Iranian president, Mahmoud Ahmadenejad, asserted that there were no homosexuals in Iran. Amnesty International reported that more than 200 people were executed in 2007 in Iran. The exact number of gays is difficult to determine because the accusations are often connected to other charges. In addition, proving that a sexual act occurred is difficult because it requires four male "righteous witnesses" to confirm the transgression.

Lesbian sex is punishable by 100 lashes. The death penalty is imposed after the fourth offense.

Going back to the 1930s in Nazi Germany more than 50,000 persons were convicted of being homosexuals. Thousands of homosexuals were tortured and killed in Nazi concentration camps. Homosexuals were persecuted in Nazi Germany on a scale unprecedented in history. In 2003 the German Bundestag voted to erect a monument in Berlin for homosexuals persecuted and murdered during the Nazi regime.

In addition to reporting on the rights of gay and lesbian citizens in the countries listed above, for example the right to marry, adopt children, serve in the military, hold certain occupational positions, we also describe the status of gay and lesbian citizens as, for example, the legality of homosexuality and sanctioned punishments. For each of the countries we ask and answer the following questions:

1. What is the history of the gay and lesbian community?
2. Is homosexuality illegal? If so, what is the punishment?
3. What rights do gays and lesbians have?

When available, pubic opinion data are reported on how respondents feel about gays and lesbians in their country as well as their opinions as to what rights should be afforded to them. Data are reported on respondents' opinions about allowing gay marriage, civil unions, adoption, and allowing gays to openly serve in the military.

Before turning to the country by country analysis, the first section reports the legal status of gay and lesbians in the countries included in the study and in those countries that impose a death sentence on persons who are gay or lesbian, in countries in which homosexuality is punishable by life imprisonment, and in an additional forty-two countries in which gays and lesbians receive prison sentences of up to twenty-five years.

The next chapters describe how the world's major religions, Christianity, Judaism, Islam, Hinduism, and Buddhism, react to homosexuality. These chapters are followed by ones that describe homosexuality in ancient Greece and Rome, the Middle Ages, Africa at the time of the arrival of Europeans, and Islamic slave traders.

We also include a chapter on how gays and lesbians are portrayed in the arts: films, plays, and literature.

The responses to homosexuality by famous psychologists including Havelock Ellis, Sigmund Freud, and Evelyn Hooker form a separate chapter.

The famous study of "tearoom trade" conducted by Laud Humphreys in which he reported the exchange of sexual favors between homosexual men in public restrooms is a separate chapter.

A discussion of the Mattachine Society, one of the first gay movement organizations in the country, is the final chapter in this section.

Part II describes the status of gays and lesbians in the twenty-one countries cited at the outset of this volume.

The country chapters are followed by an analysis of public opinion data on gay and lesbian issues in all of the countries in which national surveys had been conducted over the past thirty-five years.

Finally, Appendix A reports the treatment of homosexuals under the Nazi regime and under Stalin.

NOTES

1. Timeline of Homosexuality, available at: http://www.religionfacts.com/homosexuality/timeline.htm (October 5, 2008).

2. See *Lawrence v. Texas*, available at: http://www.law.cornell.edu/supct/html/02-102.ZS.html (October 5, 2008).

3. "Wilde libel papers go on show," available at: http://news.bbc.co.uk/1/hi/entertainment/arts/2932713.stm (October 8, 2008).

4. Ibid.

I

LEGAL, RELIGIOUS, AND HISTORICAL ANALYSES

●

Legal Status of Gays and Lesbians

The following data are based on reports from Amnesty International as of 2005. The table describes the legal status of persons who are gay or lesbian in each of the countries included in our study. The statuses range from illegal with a maximum penalty of death, to illegal with a maximum penalty of life imprisonment, to illegal with a maximum penalty of ten, seven or three years imprisonment, to illegal with a fine as a maximum penalty, to legal status.

Table 1.1: Legal Status of Gays and Lesbians in Countries Included in this Study

Country	Legal Status	Punishment
Canada	Legal for men and women	
United States	Legal for men and women	
Argentina	Legal for men and women	
Brazil	Legal for men and women	
Great Britain	Legal for men and women	
France	Legal for men and women	
Germany	Legal for men and women	
Italy	Legal for men and women	
Sweden	Legal for men and women	
Hungary	Legal for men and women	
Poland	Legal for men and women	
Russian Federation	Legal for men and women	
Iran	Illegal for men and women	Maximum penalty: Death
Israel	Legal for men and women	
Egypt	Technically legal but a variety of laws have been enacted to repress gay men	
Nigeria	Illegal for men	Maximum penalty: Death
South Africa	Legal for men and women	
India	Illegal for men and women	Maximum penalty: life imprisonment
China	Legal for men and women	
Japan	Legal for men and women	
Australia	Legal for men and women	

Table 1.2: Legal Status of Gays and Lesbians

Country	Penalty
Algeria	Maximum penalty 3 years imprisonment or a fine
Bahrain	Maximum penalty 10 years imprisonment
Botswana	Maximum penalty 7 years imprisonment
Brunei	10 years imprisonment
Cook Islands	14 years imprisonment
Cuba	Legal for men and women, but publicly manifested homosexuality is punishable by up to 1 year imprisonment
Ethiopia	3 years imprisonment
Fiji	14 years imprisonment
Gambia	14 years imprisonment
Guinea	3 years imprisonment
Jamaica	10 years of hard labor
Kenya	14 years imprisonment
Kuwait	7 years imprisonment
Lebanon	1 year imprisonment
Libya	5 years imprisonment
Malaysia	20 years imprisonment
Marshall Islands	10 years imprisonment
Mauritius	5 years imprisonment
Morocco	3 years imprisonment
Mozambique	3 years hard labor
Nicaragua	3 years imprisonment
Nepal	Illegal for men; 10 years imprisonment
Oman	3 years imprisonment
Papua New Guinea	14 years imprisonment
Qatar	5 years imprisonment
St. Lucia	25 years imprisonment
Samoa	7 years imprisonment
Senegal	5 years imprisonment
Solomon Islands	14 years imprisonment
Somalia	3 years imprisonment
Sri Lanka	10 years imprisonment
Syria	1 year imprisonment
Tanzania	14 years imprisonment
Togo	3 years imprisonment
Tokelau	Illegal for men; 10 years imprisonment
Tonga	Illegal for men; 10 years imprisonment
Trinidad & Tobago	10 years imprisonment
Tuvalu	14 years imprisonment
United Arab Emirates	14 years imprisonment
Uzbekistan	Illegal for men; 3 years imprisonment
Zambia	Illegal for men; 14 years imprisonment
Zimbabwe	Illegal for men; 3 years imprisonment

In looking over the list we note that in addition to the United States, Canada, and Australia, in all of the countries of Western Europe persons who are gay or lesbian enjoy a legal status. The only surprise on the list is India, a modern democratic society that nevertheless imposes a death sentence on persons who are gay or lesbian. Nigeria distinguishes between men and women and only imposes a death sentence on gay men.

We list below the other countries in the world not included in our study that impose a death sentence for persons who are gay or lesbian:

Afghanistan
Pakistan
Mauritania
Saudi Arabia
Sudan
Yemen

Other countries in which being gay or lesbian is illegal and punishable by life imprisonment are listed below:

Bangladesh
Bhutan
Guyana
Maldives
Nepal
Singapore
Uganda

Still additional countries in which persons who are gay or lesbian receive prison sentences of varying years are listed in table 1.2.

Of the forty-two countries listed above, six distinguish between men and women and punish only men. The range of years of imprisonment is from one to twenty-five.

❷

Christianity and Homosexuality

Christianity has a long history of oppressing gays and lesbians that traces back to the Middle Ages.[1] There are several Biblical passages cited by people who believe that God proscribes homosexuality. Some refer to the destruction of the cities of Sodom and Gomorrah from the Book of Genesis as an example of God's contempt for homosexuality that occurred within the cities: "Now before they lay down, the men of the city, the men of Sodom, both old and young, all the people from every quarter, surrounded the house. And they called to Lot and said to him, 'Where are the men who came to you tonight? Bring them out to us that we may know them carnally'" (Gen 19:4–5, NKJV). The following line from the Book of Leviticus is frequently cited as expressly prohibiting homosexual relations: "You shall not lie with a male as with a woman. It is an abomination" (Lev 18:22). A later verse explains that the punishment for such behavior is death: "If a man lies with a male as he lies with a woman, both of them have committed an abomination. They shall surely be put to death. Their blood shall be upon them" (Lev 20:13).

Some religious leaders have argued that these passages are misinterpreted or mistranslated and believe their meaning should evolve over time (e.g., contending that the cities of Sodom and Gomorrah were not destroyed solely due to homosexuality, but for larger issues of selfishness and violence).[2] Some religious leaders have a more flexible interpretation of the Bible, believing that some Biblical passages are dated and do not reflect modern attitudes on issues including homosexuality, slavery, and the treatment of women. Some passages cited to support this perspective include lines from the Book of Leviticus that read, "And as for your male and female slaves whom you may have— from the nations that are around you, from them you may buy male and female slaves. Moreover you may buy the children of the strangers who sojourn among you, and their families who are with you, which they beget in your land; and they shall become your property" (Lev 25:44–45). Another passage addressing the role of women from the Book of Deuteronomy reads, "When a man takes a wife and marries her, and it happens that she finds no favor in his eyes because he has found some uncleanness in her, and he writes her a certificate of divorce, puts it in her hand, and sends her out of his house. And when she has departed from his house she may go and be another man's wife" (Deut 24:1). Religious leaders who believe such passages from the Old Testament are out of place in modern society argue that the themes of love and redemption present most in the New Testament are what Christians should pay attention to when forming opinions on issues like homosexuality.[3]

Although most passages on homosexuality are cited from the Old Testament, there are some passages from the New Testament that are used to signify the Bible's prohibition against homosexuality. In 1 Cor 6:9 Paul writes, "Do you not know that the unrighteous will not inherit the kingdom of God? Do not be deceived. Neither fornicators, nor idolaters, nor adulterers, nor homosexuals, nor sodomites, nor thieves, nor covetous, nor drunkards, nor revilers, nor extortioners will inherit the kingdom of God." Another passage from the New Testament that is commonly cited reads, "For this reason God gave them up to vile passions. For even their women exchanged the natural use for what is against nature. Likewise also the men, leaving the natural use of the woman, burned in their lust for one another, men with men committing what is shameful, and receiving in themselves the penalty of their error which was due" (Rom 1:26-27).

In general, while Christian denominations tend to be opposed to same-sex marriage, some denominations are more accepting than others.[4] In 1992, the American Baptist church's governing body, the General Board, declared that "homosexuality is incompatible with Christian teaching." But in 2006, American Baptist churches in California, Hawaii, Nevada and Arizona broke with the national church, in reaction to the General Board's failure to penalize churches that welcomed openly gay members. The U.S. Conference of Catholic Bishops opposes gay marriage on the ground that "marriage is a faithful, exclusive and lifelong union between one man and one woman." In 2003, the conference's Administrative Committee stated that "what are called 'homosexual unions' [cannot be given the status of marriage] because they do not express full human complementarity and because they are inherently nonprocreative." Although the Episcopal Church has not explicitly established a position in favor of gay marriage, in 2006 the church stated its "support of gay and lesbian persons and [opposition to] any state or federal constitutional amendment that prohibits same-sex marriages or unions." The 2003 ordination of Gene Robinson, the church's first openly gay bishop, has caused some conservative Episcopal churches to separate from the national body. The Evangelical Lutheran Church's legislative body, the Churchwide Assembly, is expected to present its official position on the ordination of openly gay ministers and same-sex marriage in 2009 after the completion of a study on the issues. Currently, however, the Task Force for the Evangelical Church in America Studies on Sexuality defines marriage as a "lifelong and committed relationship between a man and a woman." Although the Presbyterian Church's governing body, the General Assembly, has not explicitly addressed the issue of gay marriage, it issued a ruling in 1997 prohibiting the ordination of homosexuals. Regional synods and clergy, however, have challenged this ruling, causing a major rift among Presbyterians. The Southern Baptist Convention issued a statement confirming its opposition to gay marriage. It called on "Southern Baptists not only to stand against same-sex unions but to demonstrate our love for those practicing homosexuality by sharing with them the forgiving and transforming power of the gospel of Jesus Christ." The United Methodist Church's top policymaking body, the General Conference, reaffirmed in 2004 that marriage is between a man and a woman. The church does not sanction civil unions.

In 1984, Lutherans Concerned / North America started the Reconciling in Christ (RIC) program to recognize Lutheran congregations that welcome lesbian and gay believers.[5] The list of congregations, synods, and organizations that participate in the program exceeds 300. The RIC program was initiated due to the discrimination and ignorance that many gays, lesbians, bisexuals, and transgender people face in society, including their places of worship. The RIC program seeks to make gay, lesbian, bisexual, and transgender (GLBT) members feel welcome in their congregations. A congregation, synod, or other organization joins the program in one of several ways: by having its council approve an "Affirmation of Welcome" or by having a vote of the whole congregation.[6] Once the Affirmation is adopted, the congregation, synod, or organization sends a copy of the Affirmation with a signed letter to the RIC Executive.[7] When the Affirmation is reviewed, the congregation, synod, or organization will be added to the list of RIC participants on the program's website.

As is common with social issues, opinions about same-sex marriage are closely linked with partisanship, ideology, and religion.[8] There has been a great deal of attention recently directed towards examining the foundation of people's beliefs toward same-sex marriage. In a 2004 poll, white evangelicals were found to be overwhelmingly opposed to allowing gay marriage (85 percent), and nearly three-quarters (74 percent) are opposed to civil unions, versus 61 percent and 51 percent of the general population, respectively.[9] By the term "evangelical" the survey means either respondents who indicated that they are Protestant or another Christian religious preference other than Roman Catholic, Orthodox, or Mormon and who indicated they would say they are a fundamentalist, evangelical, charismatic, or Pentecostal Protestant, or respondents who indicated that they are Protestant or another Christian religious preference other than Roman Catholic, Orthodox, or Mormon who do not consider themselves liberal or mainline and call themselves a born-again Christian. Even though white evangelicals are strongly opposed to same-sex marriage, over half (51 percent) of white evangelicals opposing gay marriage do not support amending the constitution to ban the practice, saying that state laws are sufficient.[10]

According to polls conducted by the Pew Forum on Religion and Public Life, people who attend worship services once a week or more are much more likely to oppose same-sex marriage (73 percent) than those who attend less often (43 percent opposed).[11] Opinion also varies across religions. Eighty-one percent of white evangelicals and 79 percent of black evangelicals oppose gay marriage, while Catholics and mainline Protestants are much more divided on the issue, with 48 percent of Catholics and 47 percent of mainline Protestants opposing same-sex marriage. Civil unions receive more support than same-sex marriage, with 43 percent of Protestants (30 percent of white evangelicals) and 63 percent of Catholics supporting them for same-sex couples.

According to polls conducted by the Pew Forum on Religion and Public Life in 2003, the clergy in evangelical churches give considerably more attention to homosexuality and address it far more negatively than do ministers and priests in other denominations.[12] Sixty-three percent of evangelical Protestants who attend church services at least once a month say their ministers speak out on homosexual issues, compared with 49 percent of Catholics and 33 percent of mainline Protestants. Compared with others who attend services where homosexuality is discussed, substantially more evangelicals (86 percent) say the message they are receiving is that homosexuality should be discouraged, not accepted. In addition, evangelicals who hear sermons on the issue of same-sex marriage and homosexuality are much more likely than others to believe that gays and lesbians can change their sexual orientation, and to view homosexuality as a threat to the country.

A 2004 study examining the relationship between religion and attitudes toward same-sex marriage employed logistic regression and found statistically significant results for many independent variables in their model.[13] Independent variables that were tested include religious tradition (Evangelical Protestant, African American Protestant, mainline Protestant, Catholic, Jewish, other, unaffiliated), religious practices (religious activity, friendships within congregation), demographic variables (age, education level, marital status, sex) and attitudinal measures (concern for moral values, concern about society becoming secular, and conservative ideology). The researchers found that only evangelical Protestantism and marital status are insignificant predictors of opposition to gay marriage. They noted that this finding regarding evangelical Protestantism appears counterintuitive, but point out that being a member of any religious tradition other than evangelical Protestantism (or mainline Protestantism, their reference category) increases one's likelihood of supporting gay marriage. Results also indicate that being a member of a religion other than mainstream Christianity or Judaism, or being secular, make individuals more likely to support gay marriage. Professing concern about moral values makes individuals substantially more likely to oppose gay marriage.

The researchers also tested these variables in relation to support for civil unions.[14] Here, religious tradition plays a smaller explanatory role in terms of statistical significance than it did in the gay marriage model; only being Catholic contributes significantly to the model and predicts greater support for civil unions. This might be seen as a counterintuitive direction since the Roman Catholic Church officially opposes gay marriage. Concern about moral values and conservative ideology are significant predictors of opposition to civil unions. The researchers concluded that religion is a significant influence on attitudes toward same-sex unions. Being a member of a non-Protestant religious tradition appears to lead individuals away from opposition to both gay marriage and civil unions, whereas supporting traditional attitudes on morality and secularism make individuals more likely to oppose same-sex unions.

NOTES

1. Boswell, J. (1981). *Christianity, social tolerance, and homosexuality: Gay people in western Europe from the beginning of the Christian era to the fourteenth century.* Chicago: The University of Chicago Press.

2. Public Broadcasting Service, "Christianity and homosexuality: Are they compatible?" available at: http://hem.passagen.se/nicb/christ.htm (September 3, 2008).)

3. Religious Tolerance, "Methods of interpreting the Bible," available at: http://www.religioustolerance.org/ (September 3, 2008).

4. Information on Christian denominations obtained from the Pew Forum on Religion and Public Life. "Religious Groups' Official Positions on Same-Sex Marriage," available at: http://pewforum.org/docs/?DocID=291 (August 25, 2008).

5. Lutherans Concerned/North America. "Reconciling in Christ Program," available at: http://www.lcna.org/ric.shtm (August 29, 2008).

6. Ibid.

7. Ibid.

8. The Pew Forum on Religion and Public Life. "A Stable Majority: Most Americans Still Oppose Same-Sex Marriage," available at: http://pewforum.org/docs/?DocID=290 (August 27, 2008).

9. Religion and Ethics Newsweekly. "Poll: America's Evangelicals More and More Mainstream But Insecure," available at: http://www.pbs.org/wnet/religionandethics/week733/release.html (August 27, 2008).

10. Ibid.

11. The Pew Forum on Religion and Public Life. "A Stable Majority: Most Americans Still Oppose Same-Sex Marriage," available at: http://pewforum.org/docs/?DocID=290 (August 27, 2008).

12. The Pew Forum on Religion and Public Life. "Religious Beliefs Underpin Opposition to Homosexuality," available at: http://pewforum.org/docs/index.php?DocID=37 (August 27, 2008).

13. Olson, L., Cadge, W., & Harrison, J. (2006). Religion and public opinion about same-sex marriage. *Social Science Quarterly*, 87(2), 340–60.

14. Ibid.

3

Judaism and Homosexuality

Traditional Judaism considers homosexual acts a violation of Jewish law (*halakha*).[1] Judaism's sacred texts include the Tanach, comprised of the Torah, Nevi'im, and Ketuvim, and the Talmud, which contains stories, laws, and debates about moral choices.[2] The Tanach is referred to in Christianity as the Old Testament. Therefore, the scriptural basis for rejecting homosexuality is similar in both Judaism and Christianity. Leviticus 18:22 is often cited as an example of the Bible's prohibition on homosexuality, reading, "You shall not lie with a male as with a woman. It is an abomination." The Hebrew word for "abomination" is "toevah."

Judaism is divided into several sects, or movements.[3] Orthodox Judaism is the most traditional movement; Orthodox Jews believe the entire Torah was given to Moses by God at Mt. Sinai and remains authoritative for modern life in its entirety. According to a 1990 national survey, 7 percent of American Jews are Orthodox. Reform Judaism is the most liberal expression of Judaism, with its followers believing that the Torah was inspired by God and is a living document.[4] About 1.5 million Jews in 900 synagogues are members of the Union for Reform Judaism. According to a 1990 survey, 42 percent of American Jews regard themselves as Reform. Conservative Judaism may be said to be a moderate position between Orthodox and Reform Judaism. It seeks to preserve the traditional elements of Judaism, while allowing for modernization to a more minor degree than Reform Judaism. The teachings of Zacharias Frankel (1801–1875) form the foundation of Conservative Judaism. Hasidic (or Chasidic) Judaism arose in 12th-century Germany as a mystical movement emphasizing asceticism and experience born out of love and humility before God. The modern

Hasidic movement was founded in Poland in the 18th century by Israel ben Eliezer. Reconstructionist Judaism believes that religion is an "evolving religious civilization" and does not believe in a personified deity that is active in history and does not believe that God chose the Jewish people.[5] Reconstructionists often observe Jewish Law because it is a valuable cultural remnant, rather than the Law of God.[6]

The way gay and lesbian rights are dealt with in the Jewish community depend largely on the movement. Both the Reform and Reconstructionist movements support gay and lesbian rights, including the right of same-sex couples to marry.[7] The Conservative movement does not sanctify gay marriage but grants rabbis the freedom to choose to perform same-sex marriage ceremonies. In 2007, the Conservative movement's Jewish Theological Seminary began to admit homosexuals preparing to serve as clergy.[8] This decision came about four months after the Conservative movement's law committee (The Committee on Jewish Law and Standards) adopted a position paper permitting the rabbinic ordination of gays and lesbians and allowing Conservative clergy to perform same-sex unions. The committee, however, maintained a ban on anal sex. It is left up to individual congregations to implement the decision however they choose.[9] Leaders in Orthodox Judaism have defined marriage as an institution between a man and a woman and do not permit same-sex marriage.[10] Hasidic Judaism views homosexuality as a grave sin that is taken very seriously within communities.[11]

More progressive rabbis and Jews feel that Judaism has not universally caught up to modern views on homosexuality. Some believe that it is incorrect for more traditional rabbis to ignore the American Psychiatric Association's removal of homosexuality from its list of mental illnesses in 1969 and continue to regard homosexuality as an illness.[12] In addition, many Jews believe that the translation of the word "toevah" to "abomination" is inaccurate. The other times "toevah" is used in the Bible, it is used to refer to forbidden idolatrous acts.[13] "Toevah" is also interpreted as something that is ritually unclean for Jews, like eating pork.[14]

A 2000 public opinion poll showed that Jews are more supportive of making same-sex marriage legal (55 percent compared with 26 percent of Non-Jewish respondents).[15] A 2004 study examining the relationship between religion and attitudes toward same-sex marriage employed logistic regression and found statistically significant results for many independent variables in their model.[16] Independent variables that were tested include religious tradition (Evangelical Protestant, African American Protestant, Catholic, Jewish, other, unaffiliated), religious practices (religious activity, friendships within congregation), demographic variables (age, education level, marital status, sex) and attitudinal measures (concern for moral values, concern about society becoming secular, and conservative ideology). The researchers found that being Jewish makes one substantially less likely to oppose gay marriage. Being a member of a religion other than mainstream Christianity or Judaism, or being secular, also render individuals more likely to support gay marriage. The researchers also tested these variables in relation to support for civil unions. Despite not attaining statistical significance, the values of the regression coefficient, b, indicated that being Jewish, a member of a less traditional religious group, or secular, again has substantive significance, directing individuals toward support for civil unions.

NOTES

1. Judaism and Homosexuality, available at: http://judaism.about.com/od/homosexualityandjudaism/a/samesex_2.htm (September 3, 2008).

2. Religious Tolerance. "Description of Judaism," available at: http://www.religioustolerance.org/jud_desc.htm (August 29, 2008).

3. For more information on Jewish movements, see: Religion Facts. "Jewish Denominations," available at: http://www.religionfacts.com/judaism/denominations.htm (August 29, 2008).

4. Reform Judaism, "What is Reform Judaism?" available at: http://reformjudaism.org/whatisrj.shtml (August 23, 2008).

5. Branches of Judaism, available at: http://judaism.about.com/od/denominationsofjudaism/p/branches.htm (September 12, 2008).

6. Ibid.

7. The Pew Forum on Religion and Public Life. "Religious Groups' Official Positions on Same-Sex Marriage," available at: http://pewforum.org/docs/?DocID=291 (August 25, 2008).

8. The New York Sun. "Jewish theological seminary to accept homosexuals," available at: http://www.nysun.com/new-york/jewish-theological-seminary-to-accept-homosexuals/51272/ (August 29, 2008).

9. The Jewish Daily Forward. "Conservative Panel Votes to Permit Gay Rabbis," available at: http://www.forward.com/articles/conservative-panel-votes-to-permit-gay-rabbis/ (September 10, 2008).

10. The Pew Forum on Religion and Public Life. "Religious Groups' Official Positions on Same-Sex Marriage," available at: http://pewforum.org/docs/?DocID=291 (August 25, 2008).

11. Piety, Klezmer and Queer, available at: http://www.ideasmag.artsci.utoronto.ca/issue3_2/idea&s03_02-shternshis.pdf (September 12, 2008).

12. Judaism and Homosexuality, available at: http://judaism.about.com/od/homosexualityandjudaism/a/samesex_2.htm (September 3, 2008).

13. Ibid.

14. Boswell, J. (1981). *Christianity, social tolerance, and homosexuality.* Chicago: The University of Chicago Press.

15. Maisel, L. S., Forman, I. N., Altschiller, D., & Bassett, C.W. (2001). *Jews in American politics.* Lanham, MD: Rowman & Littlefield.

16. See Olson, L., Cadge, W., & Harrison, J. (2006). Religion and public opinion about same-sex marriage. *Social Science Quarterly,* 87(2), 340-360.

4

Islam and Homosexuality

Islamic law explicitly condemns homosexuality. Same-sex marriage is prohibited in all Muslim countries; the only inconsistency is the severity of punishment for what are termed "sinful and perverted acts."[1] Same-sex intercourse is punished harshly and carries the death penalty in several Muslim nations.[2] There are some passages in the Qur'an which have been cited as addressing gay and lesbian behavior. The two main references are: "We also sent Lut: He said to his people: 'Do ye commit lewdness such as no people in creation (ever) committed before you? For ye practice your lusts on men in preference to women: ye are indeed a people transgressing beyond bounds' (Qur'an 7:80–81) and "What! Of all creatures do ye come unto the males, and leave the wives your Lord created for you? Nay, but ye are forward folk" (Qur'an 26:165). Lut is referred to as "Lot" in the Hebrew scriptures. The first passage is an implicit reference to the fall of the cities of Sodom and Gomorrah. It seems to imply that there was no homosexual behavior before it first appeared in Sodom. This is a uniquely Islamic concept; it does not appear in Jewish or Christian beliefs.[3] The passage also links the sin of Sodom to homosexuality, which led to the destruction of the city.

The Hadith are collections of sayings attributed to Muhammad. Traditional orthodox Muslims generally claim that the Hadith literature contains the authentic sayings of Muhammad, while many liberal Muslims doubt their authenticity.[4] Many hadiths discuss liwat (sexual intercourse between males).[5] Two examples are: "When a man mounts another man, the throne of God shakes" and "Kill the one that is doing it and also kill the one that it is being done to." This is believed to reference the active and passive partners in gay sexual intercourse.[6]

There is at least one mention of lesbian behavior in the Hadith: "Sihaq (lesbian sexual activity) of women is zina (illegitimate sexual intercourse) among them."[7]

The four most reliable hadith collectors and editors are Bukhari, Muslim, Abu Dawud, and Tirmidhi.[8] It is believed that when Muhammad uttered a curse against someone, it may carry eternal damnation. Muhammad cursed effeminate men and masculine women in the following hadith: "The Prophet cursed effeminate men and those women who assume the similitude of men. He also said: 'Turn them out of your houses.' He turned such and such a person out, and Umar [a principal companion of Muhammad] also turned out such and such person."[9]

While there is a consensus that same-sex intercourse is a violation of Islamic law, there are differences of opinion within Islamic scholarship about punishment, reformation, and what standards of proof are required before physical punishment becomes lawful.[10] In Sunni Islam there are four madhhabs, or legal schools, that rely mostly on analogy as a way to formulate legal rulings, and they also give different weight to the sayings of the Prophet and his companions within their decisions.[11] The four Sunni madhhabs are Hanafi, Shafi'i, Hanbali, and Maliki. The main Shia school is called Ja'fari. Each school has its own opinion on how same-sex relationships should be handled. The Hanafi school does not consider same-sex intercourse to constitute adultery and therefore leaves punishment up to the judge's discretion. Most early scholars of this school specifically ruled out the death penalty; others allowed it for a second offence. Imam Shafi'i considers same-sex intercourse to be analogous to other illegitimate sexual intercourse; thus, a married person found to have done so is punished as an adulterer (by stoning to death), and an unmarried one, as a fornicator, is left to be flogged. The Maliki school says that anyone (married or unmarried) found to have committed same-sex intercourse should be punished as an adulterer. Within the Ja'fari schools, Sayyid al-Khoi says that anyone (married or unmarried) found to have committed same-sex intercourse should be punished as an adulterer.

NOTES

1. Islamic Research Foundation International, Inc., "Same sex marriage and marriage in Islam," available at: http://www.irfi.org/articles/articles_151_200/same_sex_marriage_and_marriage_i.htm (September 8, 2008).

2. Homosexuality and Islam, available at: http://www.religionfacts.com/homosexuality/islam.htm (September 15, 2008).

3. Religions and their Attitudes to Homosexuality, available at: http://www.glcsnsw.org.au/documents/Infopack/11_religions.pdf (September 15, 2008).

4. Islam and Homosexuality, available at: http://www.missionislam.com/knowledge/homosexuality.htm (September 13, 2008).

5. Ibid.

6. Ibid.

7. Ibid.

8. Arlandson, J. "Muhammad and the homosexual," available at: http://www.answering-islam.org/Authors/Arlandson/homosexual.htm (September 13, 2008).

9. See Bukhari vol. 8, no. 6834; see vol. 7 nos. 5885 and 5886.

10. Homosexuality and Islam, available at: http://www.religionfacts.com/homosexuality/islam.htm (September 15, 2008).

11. See CRS Report for Congress, "Islam; Sunnis and Shiites," available at: http://www.fas.org/irp/crs/RS21745.pdf (September 14, 2008).

5

Hinduism, Buddhism and Homosexuality

The issue of homosexuality within Hinduism is controversial and views of homosexuality are varying and diverse, in part because the accepted Hindu religious texts do not explicitly mention homosexuality. Hinduism is the world's oldest continuously practiced religion and Hindus constitute a sixth of the world's population.[1] Most Hindus live in India but there are about 1.5 million Hindus in the United States. Modern Hindus regard all beings as manifestations of one universal *Atman* (Spirit). Homosexuality has an extensive history in India. Ancient texts like *Rig Veda*, which dates back to around 1500 BCE, sculptures, and vestiges depict sexual acts between women as revelations of a feminine world where sexuality was based on pleasure and fertility.[2]

Homosexuality is also a complex matter in Hinduism because of the many types of religious life. In general, "twice-born" Hindus (men who are of a higher caste) are prohibited from homosexual acts (*maithunam pumsi*).[3] On the other hand, the *Kama Sutra* states that homosexual sex "is to be engaged in and enjoyed for its own sake as one of the arts."[4] In general, then, the Hindu evaluation of homosexuality depends heavily on the context. The Laws of Manu is one of the standard books in the Hindu canon and is a basic text on which all gurus base their teachings. This scripture comprises 2684 verses, divided into twelve chapters presenting the norms of domestic, social, and religious life in India (circa 500 BCE) under the Brahmin influence.[5] One verse in the text says that a young woman who "pollutes" another young woman must be fined two hundred panas, pay the double of her nuptial fee, and receive ten lashes with a rod.[6] Another verse says that an adult woman who "pollutes" a young woman shall instantly have her head shaved or two fingers cut off, and be made to ride through the town on a donkey.[7] But if a man of a high caste commits an "unnatural offence" with a male, or has intercourse with a female in a cart drawn by oxen, in water, or in the daytime, shall bathe, dressed in his clothes, as his punishment.[8] Many people have criticized the Laws of Manu for heavily favoring members of the higher castes while discriminating against members of the lower castes.[9]

There are great differences amongst Hindus regarding whether homosexuality is acceptable behavior. In Hinduism, love is regarded as an eternal force. It is seen as devotion between two people, whether romantic or platonic. Hindus believe love and devotion are important in attaining Moksha—liberation from the cycle of rebirths.[10] Erotic desire or *Kama* in Hinduism was deemed as one of the most legitimate pleasures on earth (thus accounting for the vast numbers of erotic treatises, poetry, and sensuous sculptures of ancient India).[11] But this did not mean that lascivious behavior was promoted. Premarital sex in Hinduism is frowned upon and extramarital sex is prohibited. Sex was promoted within the context of a loving couple—usually heterosexual. But extremely ascetic schools of thought would have viewed sex as a distraction from the pursuit of Moksha.

Marriage in Hinduism is said to fulfill three functions: Prajaa, Dharma, and Rati.[12] In marriage, Prajaa is progeny for perpetuation of one's family, Dharma is fulfillment of responsibilities, and Rati is companionship as friends and mutual pleasure as lovers. These three functions are given in the *Dharma Shastras*, books that are not considered to be religiously binding within Hinduism. In Hinduism, many of the divinities are androgynous and some change gender to participate in homoerotic behavior. In modern India, transgendered men known as Hijras have sex with men. They religiously identify as a separate third sex, with many undergoing ritual castration. In Hindu thought, a man who penetrates a Hijra is not defined as gay. *Kama Sutra* sex acts involving homosexuality are regarded in some castes as permissible while not in other castes.[13]

Even though Hinduism does not obviously condemn homosexuality, Hindus are often intolerant of gays and lesbians. Many Hindus denounce homosexuality due to Hinduism's emphasis on the sanctity of marriage and its disapproval of premarital sex.[14] Homosexuality remains taboo in India and is legally banned in Section 377 of India's penal code. The 1996 film "Fire" which depicts a romantic relationship between two Hindu women was banned for "religious insensitivity" after a group of Hindu fundamentalists attacked cinemas where it was being screened.[15] The human rights organization People's Union for Civil Liberties has reported that sexual minorities in India face severe discrimination and violence, especially those from rural and lower caste backgrounds.[16]

Buddhism's views on homosexuality are similarly vague to those in Hinduism.[17] Buddhism has three main branches: Theravada, the oldest form of Buddhism that emphasizes the monastic life; Mahayana Buddhism, a later form that includes Zen, Nichiren, and other sects; and Vajrayana, a unique form that arose in India and Tibet and is led by the Dalai Lama. Theravada Buddhism is most commonly found in Southeast Asia and focuses on the original teachings of the Buddha. In Theravada Buddhism there are two main ways of life: the life of the monk and the life of the lay person. Buddhist monks are expected to live lives of celibacy and there is no explicit rule prohibiting gays from monastic life. Lay Buddhists, those who live outside the monastery, are expected to adhere to Five Precepts that outline ethical behavior, the third of which is a vague proscription "not to engage in sexual misconduct."

Right and wrong behavior in Buddhism is generally determined by considerations such as how it would affect others and the motivations behind the behavior. As homosexuality is not explicitly mentioned in any of the Buddha's sayings recorded in the Pali Canon (Tripitaka), many interpreters have taken this to mean that homosexuality should be evaluated in the same way as heterosexuality. Buddhism does not traditionally place great value on procreation like many other religions. From the Buddhist viewpoint, being married with children is regarded as generally positive, but not compulsory (although social norms in various Buddhist countries often have different views). Despite this, in practice, Theravada Buddhist countries are not very open to homosexuality. This has much to do with cultural norms, as well as the concept of karma, which remains strong in countries such as Thailand. From this viewpoint, a person's characteristics and situations are a result of past behavior, good or bad. Homosexuality and other alternative forms of sexuality are seen by some as karmic punishments for heterosexual misconduct in a past life.

In a 1997 interview, the Dalai Lama, the leader of Tibetan Buddhism, was asked about homosexuality. He did not offer a strong answer either way, but noted that all monks are expected to refrain from sex. For laypeople, he commented that the purpose of sex in general is for procreation, so homosexual acts do seem unnatural. He said that sexual desires are natural, perhaps including homosexual desires, but that one should not try to increase those desires or indulge them without self-control. The Dalai Lama was more specific in a meeting with Buddhist leaders and human rights activists in San Francisco in 1997, where he commented that all forms of sex other than penile-vaginal sex are prohibited for Buddhists, whether between heterosexuals or homosexuals. At a press conference the day before the meeting, he said, "From a Buddhist point of view, [gay sex] is generally considered sexual misconduct." But he did note that this rule is for Buddhists, and from society's viewpoint, homosexual relationships can be "of mutual benefit, enjoyable, and harmless." The Dalai Lama is well known for his activism for human rights, including equal rights for gays. According to an Office of Tibet spokesman, "His Holiness opposes violence and discrimination based on sexual orientation. He urges respect, tolerance, compassion, and the full recognition of human rights for all."

NOTES

1. Homosexuality and Hinduism, available at: http://www.galva108.org/hinduism.html (December 5, 2008).
2. Homosexuality and Hinduism, available at: http://www.religionfacts.com/homosexuality/hinduism.htm (December 8, 2008).
3. Ibid.
4. Ibid.
5. "The Laws of Manu," available at: http://hinduism.about.com/library/weekly/aa051303a.htm (December 8, 2008).
6. The Laws of Manu, Chapter VIII, available at: http://www.sacred-texts.com/hin/manu/manu08.htm (December 8, 2008).
7. Ibid.
8. The Laws of Manu, Chapter XI, available at: http://www.sacred-texts.com/hin/manu/manu11.htm (December 8, 2008).
9. "The Laws of Manu," available at: http://hinduism.about.com/library/weekly/aa051303a.htm (December 8, 2008).
10. Homosexuality and Hinduism, available at: http://www.religionfacts.com/homosexuality/hinduism.htm (December 8, 2008).
11. Ibid.
12. Ibid.
13. Ibid.
14. "Do Hindus Condemn Homosexuality?" Slate Magazine, available at: http://www.slate.com/id/2102443/ (December 8, 2008).
15. Trivia on "Fire," available at: http://www.imdb.com/title/tt0116308/trivia (December 8, 2008).
16. Human rights violations against sexuality minorities in India, available at: http://www.pucl.org/Topics/Gender/2003/sexual-minorities.pdf (December 8, 2008).
17. Information on Buddhism and homosexuality obtained from Homosexuality and Buddhism, available at: http://www.religionfacts.com/homosexuality/buddhism.htm (December 10, 2008).

6

Homosexuality in Ancient Greece and Rome

In ancient Greece, homosexuality was treated very differently than it is now in modern times. Greek custom did not condemn nonprocreative sex, and Greek law did not comment on same-sex relationships, except for specific prohibitions such as rape.[1] The Greeks did not find homosexuality to be a religious matter as it is often considered today. But they did pass judgment on homosexual acts and relationships in terms of their effect on social convention and on the status of Greek society's male citizens.[2] The Greek male was considered the most important member of society and was granted high rank and status over others. Any behavior that was considered to be passive or weak was not encouraged. The Greeks did not have terms or concepts to separate homosexuals and heterosexuals and attached more importance to the sexual instinct than to the sex object.[3] What most concerned the Greek male was not whether the object of desire was male or female, but what place that object occupied in the social and sexual hierarchy.[4]

There are several examples of how issues of sexuality manifested in ancient Greek writing and art. Dialogues of Plato (e.g., the *Symposium*), plays by Aristophanes, and Greek artwork and vases interpreted and presented interpretations on sexuality.[5] Greek poets wrote of same-sex love and notable philosophers and writers such as Plato, Xenophon, Plutarch, and pseudo-Lucian discussed the topic.[6] Both Alexander the Great and Zeno of Citium, the founder of Stoicism, were known for their exclusive interest in boys and other men.[7] The issue of to what gender one is attracted was seen as a matter of preference rather than as a moral issue. A character in Plutarch's *Erotikos* (*Dialogue on Love*) argues that "the noble lover of beauty engages in love wherever he sees excellence and splendid natural endowment without regard for any difference in physiological detail."[8]

As in ancient Greece, sexuality in ancient Rome was very important. Homosexuality was a part of life for most men in Rome, especially men in positions of power.[9] It was important, however, that the person in power be the active sexual partner. Being the active partner showed manliness, a prized Roman virtue, while the passive partner was perceived to be effeminate. It was acceptable for a man to have sex with both female and male prostitutes as well as slaves, as long as he was the active partner. But while slaves were seen as objects and the master could penetrate them whenever he wanted, it was looked down upon to have sex with your slave for pleasure. Rather, the act of penetration was seen as a punishment similar to a beating.[10] In ancient Rome, no religious or ethical principle made homosexual acts between men immoral or illegal. There was, however, a recognizable code that attempted to regulate sexual relations among males as closely as it regulated sexual relations between men and women.[11] The important variables were role, age, and status. For example, Roman citizens who valued their reputations did not typically have sex with each other. For a free adult male to be penetrated anally or orally by another male of any status was considered a disgrace.[12]

Ancient Rome had many parallels in its view of sexuality and same-sex relations to ancient Greece. But under the Roman Empire, society slowly became more negative in its views towards sexuality, probably due to social and economic turmoil, even before Christianity became influential.[13] One difference between ancient Rome and Greece is the practice of orgies. The Greeks practiced orgies and participated in partying more, while sexuality in Rome was somewhat more private. In ancient Rome, public bathhouses were places where homosexual behavior normally occurred. Men would scratch their head with one finger to let others know that they were looking for a sexual partner.

The Roman emperor Nero was the first emperor reported to marry a male. Of the first twelve emperors of Rome, only one, Claudius, did not have a male lover. Claudius' lack of a male lover actually drew criticism from the biographer Suetonius. While males had the ability to have both male and female lovers, female homosexual relations were not accepted in ancient Rome. Female lovers were regarded as disgusting and vile and there are reports of husbands killing their wives over homosexual affairs. With the arrival of Christianity, all forms of same-sex love became increasingly taboo. In 390, the first law banning same-sex love was enacted, making it punishable by death.[14]

NOTES

1. Fone, B. (2001). *Homophobia: A history*. New York: Picador.

2. Ibid.

3. Greek Homosexuality, available at: http://www.livius.org/ho-hz/ homosexuality/homosexuality.html (September 28, 2008); Fone, B. (2001). *Homophobia: A history*. New York: Picador.

4. Fone, B. (2001). *Homophobia: A history*. New York: Picador.

5. Homosexuality, Stanford Encyclopedia of Philosophy, available at: http://plato.stanford.edu/entries/homosexuality/ (September 30, 2008).

6. Homosexuality and the Ancient Greeks, available at: http://www .religionfacts.com/homosexuality/ancient_greeks.htm (October 1, 2008).

7. Homosexuality, Stanford Encyclopedia of Philosophy, available at: http://plato.stanford.edu/entries/homosexuality/ (September 30, 2008).

8. Ibid.

9. "Exploring Sexuality in Ancient Rome," available at: http://www. mixpills.com/history-of-sex-4-Ancient-Rome.htm (February 21, 2009).

10. Ibid.

11. Glbtq, "Ancient Rome," available at: http://www.glbtq.com/social -sciences/rome_ancient.html (February 22, 2009).

12. Ibid.

13. Homosexuality, Stanford Encyclopedia of Philosophy, available at: http://plato.stanford.edu/entries/homosexuality/ (February 20, 2009).

14. "Some historical facts about homosexuality and the law," available at: http://hrsbstaff.ednet.ns.ca/cbarre/global%20history%2012%20uploads/ some%20historical%20facts%20about%20homosexuality%20and%20gay%2 0rights.pdf (February 19, 2009).

7

Homosexuality during
the Middle Ages

There is a great deal of surviving documentation from the Middle Ages that details the existence of homosexuality during that time. While the word "homosexuality" did not exist in the Middle Ages, writers instead used the term "sodomy" to cover a range of behavior that was proscribed.[1] This term could include heterosexual anal intercourse and oral sex in addition to homosexual activity. During the Middle Ages, emotional relationships between people of the same sex were highly valued.[2] But homosexuality was frowned upon and censured. The "passive" partner in gay sex was especially reproached because it was thought to disrupt gender roles by placing a man in a stereotypically female role. Informed partly by the Catholic Church, views on the cause of homosexuality varied from beliefs that it was innate or biological, to beliefs that it resulted from an excess of general sexual desire.[3]

During the Middle Ages, the Catholic Church was staunchly against homosexuality.[4] Sodomy, whether homosexual or heterosexual, prevented conception from occurring and was therefore seen as unnatural and against God. The Church's harsh views can be seen through their penitentials—religious documents written to guide confessors on the penances to be imposed on their parishioners who admitted during confession to engaging in various sins. Several dozen of these books survive and between 4–8 percent of the penances listed are for homosexual "crimes." Virtually all of the penitentials involve long periods of penance and clearly consider homosexuality to be a major sin. Interestingly, though, some of the early medieval penitentials suggest the same period of punishment for homosexual sins as for heterosexual sins such as adultery.

But while the Church was very much against homosexuality and sodomy, its members often did not display the same conviction, as shown through their actions.[5] Churchmen were often suspected of homosexuality. Papal reformer Peter Damian tried unsuccessfully to convince the Pope that homosexuality was rife amongst priests. Historians have even suggested that some priests may have begun relationships with women to avoid the accusation of being homosexual. Priests took a vow of chastity yet many people in the Middle Ages believed that any man who was not in a relationship with a woman was either considerably less masculine or homosexual.

Anglo-Saxon vernacular and Latin writings offer some examples of how homosexuality was viewed and contrast the value and strength of male bonding to homosexual activity.[6] In *Beowulf,* the love of the older Lord Hrothgar for the young warrior Beowulf is represented in a way that might be considered homoerotic today. After Beowulf destroys both the monstrous Grendel and Grendel's mother and prepares to return to his home, the poet describes Hrothgar's longing for the young man as a desire burning powerfully in the old warrior's blood. Even though it is possible that there is an erotic subtext to this description, its context is one of masculine social affection and friendship and is approved by the Christian narrator telling this story from the ancient past.

This representation of such affection is not uncommon. In many texts, in fact, such a highly charged bond between a warrior and his lord is thought to be so powerful that its imagery is frequently invoked to describe heterosexual love.[7] But such same-sex affection differs from the homosexual expression of love. In the description of Sodom and Gomorrah in the Anglo-Saxon poem *Genesis,* there is a clear denunciation of the sodomites' desire to have sexual intercourse with two male angels as being shameful and indecent. While residing at the court of Charlemagne, English scholar Alcuin wrote and exchanged with his students homoerotic poetry in the classical tradition. But while employing powerful homoerotic imagery to emphasize male love and friendship, Alcuin explains, though certainly not as disapprovingly as the *Genesis* poet, that scholars and clerics should avoid the physical expression of such passion.

As the Middle Ages progressed, homosexuality and sodomy began to be considered as more of a secular and judicial problem than a religious one.[8] Accordingly, there were laws against homosexual acts and sodomy, with associated punishments. These varied depending on where in Europe the offences occurred and whether it was habitual or not. For example, from about 1250, death was the punishment for male homosexuality in much of Spain, France, and many of the Italian cities. It usually followed torture or castration. After 1300, male homosexuality was a capital crime in most places.

Accusations of sodomy and homosexuality were also frequently used in conjunction with charges of heresy as an excuse to charge political opponents of rulers and powerful men.[9] The most famous example of such accusations based on political motivation is the dissolution and trial of the Order of the Knights Templar. King Philip IV of France was deeply in debt to the Order and used the accusation of rampant sodomy among the Templars to arrest the vast majority of the Order in 1307. Several hundred Templars confessed that they had heard that homosexuality was permitted but that they had not engaged in it themselves. Undoubtedly Philip's strategy was an effective way to dissolve the Order, make his debts irrelevant, and a dramatic way to destroy the power of the Order who had a great deal of influence at the time.

Virtually all of the surviving sources from this time period deal with male homosexuality and male or heterosexual sodomy.[10] Accordingly, historians have paid little attention to female homosexuality. Very few of the sources, including the penitentials, discuss female homosexuality at all. There seems to have been generally less concern over lesbianism than male homosexuality, perhaps because it may have been perceived to be less common or because the authors of the works were men and therefore were naturally both more aware of and more troubled by male homosexuality. It has also been suggested that people in the Middle Ages did not take the idea seriously that sex could occur without men. But medieval lesbianism was not totally unrecorded—for instance, there was a French case involving a sixteen-year-old married woman, Laurence, and a woman named Jehanne who worked in the fields nearby. The two women were imprisoned because of their relationship.

NOTES

1. BBC, "Sodomy and Homosexuality in Medieval Europe," available at: http://www.bbc.co.uk/dna/h2g2/A7715315 (January 4, 2009).

2. GLBTQ, "English Literature: Medieval," available at: http://www.glbtq.com/literature/eng_lit1_medieval.html (January 5, 2009).

3. Ibid.

4. The following information obtained from: BBC, "Sodomy and Homosexuality in Medieval Europe," available at: http://www.bbc.co.uk/dna/h2g2/A7715315 (January 4, 2009).

5. Ibid.

6. The following information obtained from: GLBTQ, "English Literature: Medieval," available at: http://www.glbtq.com/literature/eng_lit1_medieval .html (January 5, 2009).

7. Ibid.

8. The following information obtained from: BBC, "Sodomy and Homosexuality in Medieval Europe," available at: http://www.bbc.co.uk/dna/h2g2/ A7715315 (January 4, 2009).

9. Ibid.

10. Ibid.

8

Early Africa and Homosexuality

While much of the history of homosexuality in Africa is undocumented, initial researchers claimed that Europeans or Islamic slave traders introduced homosexual behavior to African natives. In an article first published in 1974, Frances Cress Welsing argued that homosexuality was a "strategy for destroying black people."[1] Haki Madhubuti also argued that whites convinced black men to practice homosexuality in order to "disrupt black families and neutralize black men."[2] More recently, researchers have disproved these beliefs, showing that homosexual behavior appears to have developed naturally in early African society.

Anthropologists Stephen Murray and Will Roscoe reported that women in Lesotho engaged in socially sanctioned "long term, erotic relationships," called *motsoalle*.[3] They reported that this normative behavior was not thought of in a sexual manner. English anthropologist E. E. Evans-Pritchard recorded that male Azande warriors commonly took on boys between the ages of twelve and twenty who acted as wives, helping with household tasks and participating in intercrural sex with their older husbands.[4] (Intercrural sex is a type of intercourse variously regarded as penetrative and nonpenetrative sex, in which a male partner places his penis between the other partner's thighs and thrusts to create friction.) The adult males paid the families of their boys just as they paid for female brides. The practice ended after Europeans gained control of African countries.[5]

Researchers have found that in parts of Ethiopia some males cross over to feminine roles, dressing as women, performing domestic tasks, and having sexual relations with men.[6] Among Swahili speakers on the Kenya coast, *mashoga* are transgendered prostitutes who have all the liberties of men and are also welcome in many contexts in which men are prohibited. Kurt Falk wrote about an especially intimate bond of association, *soregus,* between the southeastern African Naman that included sex between both men and women.[7] Among the Tswana, lesbian practices are not prohibited and are fairly common among the older girls and young women. Use of artificial penises has also been reported among the Ila and Naman tribes of South Africa.[8]

NOTES

1. Welsing, F. C. (1991). *The Isis papers: The keys to the colors.* Chicago: Third World Press.

2. Battle, J. J., Battle, J., Bennett, M., Lemelle, A. J. (2006). Free at Last?: Black America in the Twenty-first Century. New Brunswick: Transaction Publishers.

3. Africa: Sub-Saharan, Pre-Independence, available at: http://www.glbtq .com/social-sciences/africa_pre.html (December 20, 2008).

4. Evans-Pritchard, E. E. (December, 1970). Sexual Inversion among the Azande. American Anthropologist, New Series, 72(6), 1428-1434.

5. Africa: Sub-Saharan, Pre-Independence, available at: http://www.glbtq .com/social-sciences/africa_pre.html (December 20, 2008).

6. Ibid.

7. Ibid.

8. Ibid.

9

Portrayal of Gays and Lesbians in the Arts

Gays and lesbians have been portrayed in the arts in various ways since the early nineteenth century. Perhaps Hollywood's most enduring stereotype of the gay man is the sissy.[1] The sissy exists as both a challenge to rigid masculine norms and a reinforcement of them.[2] The character is often portrayed as being close to a heterosexual male or female in a supporting role—a faithful friend, valet, or decorator.[3] Early examples of this stereotype are shown in *The Celluloid Closet* (1926) and *Movie Crazy* (1932). One character in *Movie Crazy* exemplifies this effeminate stereotype by shrieking and leaping onto a table at the thought of a mouse.[4] In *The Gay Divorcee* (1934), Edward Everett Horton plays Fred Astaire's friend nicknamed "Pinky" who appears over-emotional and engages in conspiratorial behavior with Astaire. In *Bed of Roses* (1933), a character is portrayed as the head of a women's department in a clothing store.[5] Another less-popular stereotype is the tragic homosexual. In such films as *Dracula's Daughter* (1936), *Rebecca* (1940), *Rebel without a Cause* (1955) and *Strangers on a Train* (1951), the tragic homosexual holds a role of minor importance and is portrayed as desperate and searching out love and happiness or victims, as in movies in the thriller genre.[6] *The Children's Hour* (1961), starring Audrey Hepburn and Shirley MacLaine, was the first major Hollywood film depicting lesbianism and the first with a major, obviously lesbian, character.[7] Due to the controversial subject matter, the movie was considered a challenge to the Hays Code of 1930, which governed the content of movies, and resulted in the revision of the code to permit "tasteful treatments of homosexual themes."[8] *The Children's Hour* was originally a play that first appeared on Broadway in 1934. Although well received by critics, the play was banned in

Chicago, Boston, and London. The Pulitzer Prize committee refused to consider it for its award.

Rope, a film directed by Alfred Hitchcock in 1948, was inspired by the Leopold and Loeb murder case of 1924 and accurately portrayed the two men as gay. Hitchcock subtly wove hints of their sexuality throughout the film; in actuality, Leopold and Loeb's gay relationship came out in their murder trial and was used as a sign of their insanity. At the time of *Rope*, it was uncommon to speak frankly about homosexuality and the movie's indirect suggestions evidence that tone of society. It was not until a 1992 adaptation of the story that filmmakers explicitly displayed Leopold and Loeb's sexual relationship.[9] Leopold and Loeb, both extremely intelligent and students at the University of Chicago, were convicted of murdering a 14-year-old boy and were both sentenced to life imprisonment. Leopold and Loeb were driven to commit the crime by Nietzsche's idea of the "superman"—that there are some people in society who are morally superior to others and therefore are able to commit crime. Leopold and Loeb were also motivated by their fascination with and desire to commit the perfect crime. Leopold and Loeb acted as accomplices, with Loeb agreeing to perform sexual favors for Leopold in return for his cooperation in their plans. There was a great public outcry in response to the murder and the public's interest in the case still exists over 80 years after the crime.

James Baldwin was a popular writer during the era of civil rights activism and regularly included gay themes in his work. Baldwin was openly gay and became increasingly outspoken on issues of discrimination.[10] At the age of fourteen he became a preacher in his stepfather's Fireside Pentecostal Church, and though he left the ministry when he was eighteen, the style and cadences of the Pentecostal pulpit remained as a feature of his writing.[11] From 1948 until his death he spent much of his time abroad, and the distance provided him with the perspective he needed to write about his life experiences being both gay and African-American in America.[12] In an early essay titled "The Preservation of Innocence," Baldwin discusses the legitimacy of homosexual desire. One of his best-known novels, *Go Tell It on the Mountain* (1953), is an autobiography that details his struggle to forge an identity contrary to what is expected of him by others.[13] *Giovanni's Room* (1956) more openly discusses issues of homosexuality, focusing on the consequences of being unwilling to accept a homosexual identity.[14] The book centers on the narrator, David, who is torn between his fiancée Hella and his lover. His confusion mirrors that of many gay men during the 1950s.[15] *Giovanni's Room* was one of the first American novels to deal with the topic of homosexuality and drew criticism from some who thought it was too candid.[16] Many of his books featuring gay themes drew strong criticism within the African-American community and challenged societal norms. His writings preceded the famous Stonewall Riots of 1969 and, while controversial at the time, opened the door for homosexuality to be discussed in modern literature.[17]

NOTES

1. Glbtq, "Film," available at: http://www.glbtq.com/arts/film,2.html (October 18, 2008).

2. Glbtq, "Film Sissies," available at: http://www.glbtq.com/arts/film_sissies.html (October 18, 2008).

3. Ibid.

4. Glbtq, "Film," available at: http://www.glbtq.com/arts/film,2.html (October 18, 2008).

5. Glbtq, "Film Sissies," available at: http://www.glbtq.com/arts/film_sissies.html (October 18, 2008).

6. Glbtq, "Film," available at: http://www.glbtq.com/arts/film,2.html (October 18, 2008).

7. Hadleigh, B. (2001). *The Lavender Screen.* New York: Citadel Press.

8. "The Motion Picture Production Code of 1930 (Hays Code)," available at: http://www.artsreformation.com/a001/hays-code.html (October 24, 2008); "The Children's Hour," available at: http://www.nyu.edu/classes/jeffreys/gaybway/gayhollywood/ChildrensHour.htm (October 24, 2008).

9. Glbtq, "Screenwriters," available at: http://www.glbtq.com/arts/screen-writers,2.html (October 17, 2008).

10. University of Illinois at Chicago, "James Baldwin," available at: http://www.uic.edu/depts/quic/history/james_baldwin.html (October 17, 2008).

11. "James Baldwin," available at: http://sunsite.berkeley.edu/gaybears/baldwin/ (October 23, 2008).

12. Ibid.

13. University of Illinois at Chicago, "James Baldwin," available at: http://www.uic.edu/depts/quic/history/james_baldwin.html (October 17, 2008).

14. Ibid.

15. "James Baldwin," available at: http://sunsite.berkeley.edu/gaybears/baldwin/ (October 23, 2008).

16. Ibid.

17. Glbtq, "James Baldwin," available at: http://www.glbtq.com/literature/baldwin_j.html (October 17, 2008).

🔟

Early Psychology and Homosexuality

Havelock Ellis, British psychologist and writer, was one of the first modern thinkers to challenge taboos against the frank and open discussion of sex.[1] In 1896, Ellis published the first part of what became a seven-volume series titled *Studies in the Psychology of Sex*. The book, under the title *Sexual Inversion*, was not well received upon its 1897 publication in England with coauthor John Symonds. Symonds' family was unhappy with its frankness and Symonds' literary executor withdrew his permission for Ellis to cite Symonds and attempted to buy up the entire printing for destruction.[2] As a result, the book was reissued under Ellis's name alone, with Symonds referred to only as "Z."[3] In *Sexual Inversion*, Ellis cited many reports of same-sex behaviors among animals and people of diverse cultures, concluding that homosexuality is both natural and, in ideal circumstances, a valid expression of love between two like-minded adults.[4] In his writings, Ellis advocated women's rights to sexual fulfillment and, shortly after the Oscar Wilde trial, he voiced his opposition to criminalizing homosexual acts.[5]

Sigmund Freud is famous for the founding of psychoanalysis and his writings on the human unconscious. Freud's theories have had a significant impact on the study of psychology and his tolerant attitude on homosexuality was unique for his time. Freud incorporated sexuality into many of his theories, believing that it was at the core of human functioning. Although Freud believed that heterosexuality was the most appropriate sexual orientation due to its propagation of the species, he also said that "homosexuality is assuredly no advantage, but it is nothing to be ashamed of, no vice, no degradation, it cannot be classified as an illness."[6] Freud has also been quoted as saying that homosexuality is considered to be "a variation of the sexual function, produced by a certain arrest of sexual development" and that attempting to transform a fully developed homosexual into a heterosexual would be as unlikely as transforming a heterosexual into a homosexual.[7] Freud also believed that bisexuality was something fundamental to all humans—latent in heterosexuals and an explanatory principle of homosexuality.

American psychologist Evelyn Hooker's pioneering studies on male homosexuality in the 1950s and 1960s challenged the model of homosexuality that, at that time, regarded homosexuality as a disease. Through her research and advocacy efforts, she is famous for helping to spur the modern gay rights movement. In 1954, she received a grant from the National Institute for Mental Health that led to her breakthrough study published in 1957.[8] For her study, Hooker administered standard psychological exams—accepted by professionals as indicators of the presence of emotional and mental disorders—to men with the purpose of determining whether conventional wisdom regarding the pathology of homosexuality was true. She administered three personality tests, including the Rorshach ink-blot test, to thirty pairs of men—one homosexual, one not—matched by IQ level, age, and other factors.[9] Hooker gave the test results to a panel of three prominent experts, asking them to diagnose which of the sixty men had a psychiatric disorder and which of the men in each pair was homosexual. The experts concluded that the gay males were no worse, and sometimes better adjusted than the rest, and proved unable to identify correctly the gay male in each pair.[10]

The results suggested the assumption that homosexuals were necessarily psychiatrically disordered is erroneous and also suggested that any diagnoses of disorder may be based more on stereotypes and researcher biases rather than on objective fact.[11] Many of Hooker's colleagues who subscribed to "sickness" theories of homosexuality challenged her methods and conclusions. Later in her career, Hooker was appointed the Chair of the National Institute of Mental Health's Task Force on Homosexuality. In 1967, the Task Force issued a report that was severely critical of attempts to "treat" homosexuality and led to the rescinding of homosexuality from the American Psychiatric Association's *Diagnostic and Statistical Manual of Psychiatric Disorders* in 1973.[12]

NOTES

1. Glbtq, "Havelock Ellis," available at: http://www.glbtq.com/social-sciences/ellis_h.html (November 9, 2008).

2. Ibid.

3. Ibid.

4. Ibid.

5. Ibid.

6. Glbtq, "Sigmund Freud," available at: http://www.glbtq.com/social-sciences/freud_s.html (November 7, 2008).

7. Ibid.

8. Glbtq, "Evelyn Hooker," available at: http://www.glbtq.com/social-sciences/hooker_e.html (November 6, 2008).

9. Ibid.

10. Ibid.

11. Ibid.

12. Ibid.

⑪

Tearoom Trade

Laud Humphreys, a student sociologist who was attempting to earn his PhD at Washington University in the 1960s, made the idea of "tearoom trade" famous.[1] Humphreys began researching what he referred to as "tearoom trade," or the exchange of sexual favors between two anonymous men in public restrooms. He used the work of Evelyn Hooker as his theoretical foundation, with the goal of understanding this behavior and to determine a classification for particular sexual behaviors. Humphreys focused primarily on restrooms in public parks and frequented restrooms to observe these behaviors. He offered to serve as a "watchqueen" for the men so they would avoid detection by the police or strangers. Humphreys wanted to track the people he observed so he would write down the license plates of the men's vehicles. He obtained the men's home addresses and, after one year, went to their houses in disguise in order to interview them, posing as a social health interviewer. Through these interviews, Humphreys determined that over 50 percent of the men did not consider themselves homosexuals and were mostly happily married and had responsibilities in their communities.

As a result of his research, Humphreys identified five types of homosexuals: adolescent male hustlers, ambisexuals, closet queens, gay guys and trade homosexuals. Humphreys was unable to gain the support of many of his academic colleagues due to the level of deception and dishonesty in his study. As a result of this perceived dishonesty, the Sociology Department at Washington University rescinded his PhD. Some researchers, however, view his work to be groundbreaking and a significant addition to the field. There is some indication that Humphreys' research helped persuade police departments to stop using their resources to make arrests for this victimless crime.[2]

Although Humphreys' controversial research made tearoom trades well known to the public, tearooms had been under police scrutiny since the opening of public facilities in 1896.[3] In 1920, management at the Boise Valley Traction Company hired one of its employees to spy through a hole in the men's room ceiling. His surveillance resulted in the arrest and conviction of two men, who were sentenced to five years each in the Idaho State Prison.[4] Entrapment was frequently used to police tearoom sex. As early as the 1910s in New York, plainclothes officers entered park toilets and subway washrooms, pretending to be cruising for sex.[5] In some cases, police decoys blackmailed men for money in return for letting the men go without being arrested.

One of the most famous tearoom arrests in U.S. history took place in October 1964. That month, the District of Columbia's vice squad began conducting surveillance of the basement restroom of the YMCA on G Street, two blocks from the White House.[6] Spying through peepholes in the locked door of an unused shower room, police officers caught two men engaging in sexual acts. One of the men was Walter Jenkins, chief of staff to President Lyndon B. Johnson. President Johnson ordered the FBI to conduct a full investigation of Jenkins's activities while in office. The 100-page "Report on Walter Wilson Jenkins," released at the end of October, concluded that the former chief of staff had never "compromised the security or interests of the United States."[7]

NOTES

1. See McMurry University, "Laud Humphreys," available at: http://www.mcm.edu/~dodd1/TWU/FS5023/Humphreys.htm (October 22, 2008); Humphreys, L. (1975). *Tearoom trade: Impersonal sex in public places.* New York: Aldine Transaction.

2. "Laud Humphreys and the Tearoom Sex Study," available at: http://web.missouri.edu/~bondesonw/Laud.html (October 26, 2008).

3. Tearoom History, available at: http://www.planetout.com/news/history/archive/10251999.html (October 25, 2008).

4. Ibid.

5. Ibid.

6. Ibid.

7. Ibid.

⑫

The Mattachine Society and New York City's Stonewall Inn

One of the first gay movement organizations in the United States was the Mattachine Society, started in Los Angeles in 1950.[1] Harry Hay formed the organization along with seven other men with the goal of redefining the meaning of being gay in the U.S. The Society's name comes from a French medieval masque group called "Société Mattachine" which symbolized the gay population's feeling of being a masked, unknown group.[2] In 1951, the Mattachine Society adopted a Statement of Missions and Purpose, which both recognized the importance of building a gay community and called for gays to challenge anti-gay discrimination. Although often gathering in secret, the Society provided its members with an open forum, sponsoring discussion groups for gays and lesbians to share their feelings and experiences. The Society came under public scrutiny in the early 1950s due to the Communist leanings of several of its founders and the group's political actions, including protesting police entrapment of gay men.[3] The Society held member conventions which led to the resignation of the original founders, due to members' beliefs that the group might be subject to a government investigation. The leaders who took over the Society restructured the group's goals and advocated accommodation over social change. These changes led to the decline of the group's membership and attendance, resulting in the dissolution of the Society's national structure in 1961.[4] While some chapters remained active, other organizations like the Gay Liberation Front became more dominant in the gay liberation movement. The final Mattachine Society office closed in the 1980s.[5]

The first national lesbian organization in the United States, the Daughters of Bilitis (DOB), was founded in San Francisco in 1955 and was influenced by the Mattachine Society. The Daughters of Bilitis began when a lesbian couple, Phyllis Lyon and Del Martin, began meeting with other female couples to discuss lesbian issues. The Daughters of Bilitis believed the group's name would be both subtle enough that the general public would be unaware of its meaning while knowledgeable lesbians would understand. The group's activities included hosting public forums on homosexuality, offering support to isolated and married lesbians, and participation in research activities.

Shortly after the breakdown of the Mattachine Society, an incident at the Stonewall Inn in New York City served as the catalyst for the brewing gay activist movement. The Stonewall Inn on Christopher Street was a popular gay bar, a rare place where people of the gay community could gather and socialize openly. In 1969, police raided the Stonewall Inn and threw the patrons out of the bar, arresting the bartender, doorman, and some patrons.[6] But the other patrons fought back and gathered on the street protesting; the protesting group grew and eventually numbered around 2,000 people.[7] Police reinforcements arrived and drove away the crowd. The crowd returned the next night and rioted in the street outside the inn for two hours. The police sent in a riot-control squad to disperse the group. Approximately 1,000 protestors returned to the street days later and continued the protest and march on Christopher Street.[8]

The incident at the Stonewall Inn was a pivotal moment in the gay rights movement, uniting the gay community in New York in the fight against discrimination. The following year, a march was organized in commemoration of the Stonewall riots and between 5,000 and 10,000 men and women attended.[9] In honor of Stonewall, many gay pride celebrations around the world are held during the month of June, including New York City's Pride Week.[10] Still today, the Stonewall Inn is a popular favorite gay night spot in New York City.

NOTES

1. Mattachine Society, available at: http://www.glbtq.com/social-sciences/mattachine_society.html (October 12, 2008).

2. Ibid.

3. Ibid.

4. Ibid.

5. Harry and the Mattachine Society, available at: http://www.harryhay.com/AH_matt.html (October 11, 2008).

6. Historic Stonewall Place, available at: http://www.stonewall-place.com/ (October 10, 2008).

7. Ibid.

8. Ibid.

9. The Stonewall Riots, available at: http://manhattan.about.com/od/glbtscene/a/stonewallriots.htm (October 12, 2008).

10. Ibid.

II

REPORT ON GAYS AND LESBIANS
Country By Country

⓭

Canada

In 2005, Canada passed the Civil Marriage Act and became the fourth country to legalize same-sex marriage after the Netherlands, Belgium, and Spain.[1] The parliament inserted a provision in the bill recognizing that religious officials were not obligated to perform same-sex marriage ceremonies if it went against their religion's beliefs.[2] Canada's history with gays and lesbians before legalizing same-sex marriage was relatively liberal. Although after World War II male homosexuality was initially prohibited and the social climate was somewhat hostile towards gays and lesbians, the political climate soon changed.[3] The 1966 conviction for homosexuality of Everett Klippert sparked public debate in Canada over laws criminalizing homosexuality.[4] In 1969, the Prime Minister passed an amendment that decriminalized homosexuality.[5] Additionally, in 1977, Quebec became the first province to include "sexual orientation" in its human rights legislation and in 1978, Canada's Immigration Act was amended to remove a ban on homosexuals as immigrants.[6] Furthermore, in 1988, a Canadian church allowed gays to be ordained.[7] In 2002, the British Columbia Anglican Church issued a proclamation in favor of blessing civil union ceremonies.[8] Prior to passage of the Civil Marriage Act, several provinces had already extended marriage rights to same-sex couples.[9] Over 12,000 civil marriage licenses have been issued to gay and lesbian couples since licenses began to be issued in the Ontario province on June 10, 2003.[10]

Gays and lesbians are afforded many rights in Canada. The Criminal Code of Canada covers gays and lesbians under its hate crime statute and the Canadian Human Rights Act of 1985 prohibits discrimination based on sexual orientation.[11] Since 1992, gays and lesbians have been permitted to openly serve in the military, live with their partners on military bases, and are eligible to receive pensions from their same-sex partners.[12] The Canadian military performed its first same-sex marriage ceremony in Nova Scotia in 2005.[13] Canada is unique because both citizens and noncitizens may sponsor a same-sex partner on their application for permanent resident status.[14] One noncitizen must qualify to immigrate based on Canada's points system and can then sponsor his or her partner based on "humanitarian and compassionate" grounds.[15] Previous laws allowed for the immigration of same-sex partners with special permission from an immigration official.[16] In addition, Canada grants asylum to gays and lesbians who have been or are expected to be persecuted in their home countries because of their sexual orientation.[17]

Although gays and lesbians have many rights under Canadian law, transsexuals have been discriminated against in the workplace, social life, and even in the prison system.[18] Many complaints have been filed alleging that employers discriminated against transsexuals both in their hiring processes and on the job.[19] Canadian prisons have dealt with issues of housing, medical treatment, and treatment of transsexuals by fellow inmates. Transsexuals are often housed without consideration of their gender identity, are refused sex reassignment surgery, and are often not given counseling or hormone therapy.[20] In 2001, Synthia Kavanagh filed a complaint with the Canadian Human Rights Commission (CHRC) because of the treatment she received as a transsexual inmate.[21] She won her case and the ruling stated that the housing needs of transsexuals should be assessed individually, prison officials should protect transsexuals from sexual attacks and harassment, and sex reassignment surgery should be easier to obtain when it was recommended by a person's physician before entering jail or prison.[22]

PUBLIC OPINION DATA[23]

In a 2007 poll, 70 percent of respondents believed that homosexuality should be accepted and 21 percent believed that it should be rejected.[24] A slight majority of Canadian respondents supported allowing gays and lesbians to marry legally, 53 percent in 1999, but in 2001 only 45 percent said they supported gays and lesbians to marry legally. In addition, the majority favors the authorization of child adoption by same-sex couples (53 percent in 2001) and equal tax breaks for couples irrespective of their sexual orientation (74 percent in 2001). Furthermore, in 1987, 63 percent indicated support

Table 13.1:   Do you agree or disagree with the following? (In Percent)

Canada		Agree	Disagree	Total (N)
Legal recognition of same-sex marriage				
	1999	53	44	97 (N/A)
	2001	45	47	92 (N/A)
Authorization of child adoption by homosexual couples				
	2001	53	47	100 (N/A)
Equal tax breaks for both heterosexual and same-sex couples				
	2001	74	26	100 (N/A)
Equal rights in jobs and housing				
	1987	63	37	100 (N/A)
Custody rights for lesbian mothers				
	1987	72	28	100 (N/A)
Equal rights for gay and lesbian teachers				
	1987	51	49	100 (N/A)

for equal rights in jobs and housing, 72 percent supported custody rights for lesbian mothers, and 51 percent supported equal rights for gay and lesbian teachers.

NOTES

1. Catholic News Agency, available at: http://www.catholicnewsagency .com/new.php?n=4433 (July 7, 2008).

2. Parliament of Canada, Bill C-38, available at: http://www2.parl.gc.ca/ HousePublications/Publication.aspx?Language=E&Parl=38&Ses=1&Mode=1 &Pub=Bill&Doc=C-38_4 (May 13, 2008).

3. Adam, B. (1993). "Winning rights and freedoms in Canada." In *The Third Pink Book*, eds. A. Hendriks, R. Tielman, & E. Veen. Buffalo, NY: Prometheus Books.

4. Mapleleafweb, Same Sex Marriage in Canada, available at: http://www .mapleleafweb.com/features/same-sex-marriage-canada (June 25, 2008).

5. Chronology : Same-Sex Marriage, available at:http://www.canada .com/national/story.html?id=41a2cfbb-5124-4527-8627-3af8aa1919de (June 28, 2005).

6. Mapleleafweb, Same Sex Marriage in Canada, available at: http://www .mapleleafweb.com/features/same-sex-marriage-canada (June 25, 2008).

7. Ibid.

8. Gay Law Net, available at: http://www.gaylawnet.com/ (April 26, 2008).

9. Equal Marriage for Same-Sex Couples, available at: http://www .samesexmarriage.ca/ (May 13, 2008).

10. Canadians for Equal Marriage, available at: http://www.equal-marriage .ca/resource.php?id=500 (May 13, 2008).

11. Criminal Code of Canada, available at: http://laws.justice.gc.ca/en/ C-46/ (May 13, 2008); Canadian Human Rights Commission, available at: http://www.chrc-ccdp.ca/legislation_policies/human_rights_act-en.asp (June 25, 2008).

12. Gay Law Net, available at: http://www.gaylawnet.com/ (April 26, 2008); Mapleleafweb, Same Sex Marriage in Canada, available at: http://www .mapleleafweb.com/features/same-sex-marriage-canada (June 25, 2008).

13. Ibid.

14. Citizenship and Immigration, available at: http://www.cic.gc.ca/english/ information/applications/guides/5289E2.asp (June 27, 2007).

15. Partners Task Force for Gay and Lesbian Couples, available at: http:// buddybuddy.com/immigr.html (May 16, 2008).

16. Canadians for Equal Marriage, available at: http://www.equal-marriage .ca/resource.php?id=500 (May 13, 2008).

17. Partners Task Force for Gay and Lesbian Couples, available at: http:// buddybuddy.com/immigr.html (May 16, 2008).

18. Barbara Findlay, Transsexuals in Canadian prisons: An equality analysis, available at: http://www.barbarafindlay.com/articles/45.pdf (July 2, 2008).

19. Ibid.

20. Ibid.

21. Prison Justice, Resources on Transsexual/Transgendered People in Prison, available at: http://www.prisonjustice.ca/starkravenarticles/trans_in_ prison_0706.htrml (July 2, 2008).

22. Ibid.

23. See Canadian Public Polls on Homosexuality, available at: http://www .religioustolerance.org/hom_poll4.htm (May 13, 2008); Sniderman, P. et al., *The clash of rights: Liberty, equality, and legitimacy in pluralist democracy.* New Haven: Yale University Press.

24. Pew Global Attitudes Project, "World publics welcome global trade— but not Immigration," available at: http://pewglobal.org/reports/display .php?ReportID=258 (November 21, 2008).

United States

HISTORY

Procreation dominated the social attitude toward sexuality for the North American settlers who migrated from England in the seventeenth and eighteenth centuries.[1] The production of children was a necessity as settlers were creating colonies and desiring to sustain life for a next generation. The idea of heterosexuality was undefined due to it being the only way of life publicly known and acknowledged. Although records indicate that men and women engaged in sexual activity with members of the same sex, nothing indicates that they thought of themselves as "homosexual."[2] Homosexual acts were sanctioned with other sexual deviations like adultery and people were understood to be practicing a vice rather than manifesting an identity or a pathology.[3] As early as 1624, the colony of Virginia executed a ship's master for homosexual acts and the New Haven colony prescribed the death penalty for same-sex relations between women in 1656.[4]

By the American Revolution, Thomas Jefferson and a group of reformers had suggested a revision of Virginia's law that would have eliminated the death penalty for sodomy and substituted castration for it.[5] With the emergence of capitalism in the later half of the nineteenth century, it became possible for people to have autonomous lives outside of a family.[6] Only in the nineteenth century did experts begin to speak of "the homosexual" as someone whose erotic desire reflected an unusual physiological or psychological condition.[7] From the 1870s through 1930s, groups of people recognized their attraction to members of the same sex and felt this identification made them different from others. Many met in saloons and clubs and did not attempt to conceal their sexual identity while gathering in controlled settings.[8] Police responded to this new subculture by arresting people on charges of disorderly conduct, vagrancy, public lewdness, and assault.[9]

The issue of when gays and lesbians began to define themselves as such is typically seen as a phenomenon of the last seventy-five to a hundred years, mostly confined to the Western world.[10] Many researchers argue that before about the mid-nineteenth century, no one would have understood our current conception of homosexual behavior as being organized around a self-conscious sexual identity and a behavioral pattern which emphasizes the exclusion of opposite-gender attraction.[11] The scientific community proclaimed that homosexuality was both a disease and hereditary. It was not until 1973 that homosexuality was taken off the list of mental disorders listed in the *Diagnostic and Statistical Manual of Mental Disorders* (DSM).[12]

The 1960s and 1970s saw the emergence of gay and lesbian activism and increasing public awareness about homosexuality. In 1962, Illinois became the first U.S. state to decriminalize private homosexual acts between consenting adults. The civil rights movement and anti–Vietnam War protests left many gay activists with the desire to create an organized movement.[13] By the mid 1970s, homosexuals and lesbians had formed more than 1,000 organizations around the country.[14]

The rights of gay and lesbian citizens in the United States has been a salient issue in recent years, seen through both the amount of legislation addressing the issue and its presence on presidential candidates' platforms. Many changes in laws and policies have happened only in recent years. For example, in 1973, the American Psychiatric Association removed homosexuality from its list of mental disorders.[15] Many advocacy groups and politicians have attempted to change federal laws regarding the legal rights of same-sex couples. In 2006, a proposal for a constitutional amendment banning gay marriage was rejected by the U.S. Congress.[16] In 1996, the Defense of Marriage Act (DOMA) was passed which allows states the freedom to choose if they will recognize same-sex marriages from other states. DOMA also defines "marriage" and "spouse" in federal law; marriage being the legal union of a man and woman and a spouse being the husband or wife of the opposite sex.[17] Some argue that the Act violates the full faith and credit clause of the Constitution that requires each state to honor the laws of other states.[18]

The treatment of gays and lesbians has evolved over the years. In the 1940s and 1950s, homosexuality was seen as a pervasive weakness that opened the United States to Communist influences.[19] In the late 1950s and 1960s, bad parenting was often blamed for a child's sexuality. During this time, Americans were exposed to homosexuality in the context of a "moral panic." News reports sensationalized government crackdowns and presented homosexuality as a threat to society and morality.[20] In the 1970s, many Americans viewed gays and lesbians as immoral, misguided, and ill. A 1977 poll showed that Americans were least likely to support laws protecting gays and lesbians against job discrimination compared to other minority groups.[21] Recently, states have wrestled with the decision of allocating rights to gays and lesbians, particularly the right of marriage.

Many states afford gay and lesbian citizens different rights. In 1962, Illinois became the first state to decriminalize homosexual acts between consenting adults in private.[22] In 1982, Wisconsin became the first state to outlaw discrimination on the basis of sexual orientation.[23] In 2000, Vermont became the first state to legally recognize same-sex civil unions. Connecticut followed in 2005 and New Jersey in 2006.[24] In 2004, Massachusetts began issuing marriage licenses to same-sex couples as a result of the court's ruling that barring gays and lesbians from marrying violates the state constitution.[25] In 2008, a New York State appeals court voted that valid same-sex marriages performed in other states must be recognized by employers in New York, granting same-sex couples the same rights as other couples.[26] Also in 2008, Oregon passed a law that allows same-sex couples to register as domestic partners, granting them some spousal rights of married couples. The California Supreme Court also ruled in 2008 that same-sex couples have a constitutional right to marry.[27] California began issuing marriage licenses to same-sex couples in June 2008. Although California and Massachusetts are the only states that allow same-sex couples to marry, Rhode Island recognizes same-sex marriages from other states.[28] In addition, Connecticut, Vermont, New Jersey, and New Hampshire provide for civil unions and Hawaii, Maine, the District of Columbia, Washington, and Oregon provide rights to same-sex couples through domestic partnerships.[29] In December 2008, the California Supreme Court accepted three lawsuits seeking to nullify Proposition 8, a constitutional amendment approved by voters in the November 2008 election.[30] The passage of Proposition 8 overruled the court's decision in May 2008 that legalized gay marriage. The three cases claim the measure abridges the civil rights of a vulnerable minority group. They argue that voters alone did not have the authority to enact such a significant constitutional change. Oral arguments for the case began on March 5, 2009; however, gay couples are not permitted to marry until the court rules. The court must issue its decision within ninety days of oral arguments.[31]

There have been many recent U.S. Supreme Court cases addressing the rights of gays and lesbians. The 1986 case of *Bowers v. Hardwick* held that gays do not have a fundamental right to engage in sodomy.[32] In the 1998 case of *Oncale v. Sundowner Offshore Services, Inc.*, the U.S. Supreme Court held that sexual harassment by persons of one sex against persons of the same sex is actionable under Title VII.[33] In the 2000 case of *Boy Scouts of America v. Dale*, the U.S. Supreme Court ruled that a New Jersey antidiscrimination law that required the Boy Scouts of America to admit an openly gay man as a scoutmaster violated the Boy Scouts' first amendment right of expressive association.[34] In 2003, the Supreme Court ruled in *Lawrence v. Texas* that a Texas law that prohibited sexual acts between same-sex couples was unconstitutional. The Court held that the right to privacy protects a right for adults to engage in private, consensual homosexual activity and overruled *Bowers v. Hardwick*.[35]

Although most states and the federal government do not have laws prohibiting discrimination based on sexual orientation, in 1998 President Clinton issued an executive order prohibiting such discrimination in federal civilian employment.[36] In 2003, the U.S. Circuit Court of Appeals in San Francisco ruled that schools failing to protect gay students from harassment could be in violation of federal law.[37] The court held that a school must take steps to eliminate harassment when it learns that lesbian, gay, and bisexual students are abused at school.[38] All but five states—Arkansas, Georgia, Indiana, South Carolina, and Wyoming—have hate crime laws based on sexual orientation or gender identity.[39]

Gays and lesbians, especially same-sex partners, are often not treated in the same manner as opposite-sex couples. For tax purposes, gay and lesbian couples must file individually even if their incomes are combined. Same-sex couples are therefore taxed more heavily than married couples who are taxed jointly.[40] In 2005, the George W. Bush administration rewrote the rules governing the adjudication of security clearances. Previous language stated that a person's sexual orientation "may not be used as a basis for or a disqualifying factor in determining a person's eligibility for a security clearance." The language was rewritten to say that security clearances cannot be denied "solely on the basis of the sexual orientation of the individual."[41] In 2002, President Bush signed legislation allowing death benefits of public safety officers killed on September 11, 2001 to go to a beneficiary other than an immediate family member. This is believed to be the first time federal benefits have been available to survivors in gay partnerships.[42]

The United States currently does not give same-sex couples benefits in terms of immigration. The Uniting American Families Act (UAFA), first introduced in 2000, would let U.S. citizens and permanent residents sponsor their foreign-born partners applying for U.S. citizenship.[43] The bill has been reintroduced in congressional sessions several times after having failed to pass. Senator Patrick Leahy most recently reintroduced the bill in 2009.[44] Under current law, an American citizen is permitted to sponsor his or her spouse for a green card under the family immigration system. The UAFA would extend this right to same-sex couples by adding "or permanent partner" to sections of the Immigration and Naturalization Act that apply to legally married couples. Under the proposed legislation, a "permanent partner" is described as an adult who is in a committed, intimate, financially interdependent relationship with another adult in "which both parties intend a lifelong commitment." The United States does grant asylum to gay and lesbians from other countries who are persecuted for their sexual orientation.[45]

The military currently operates under a policy known as "Don't Ask, Don't Tell." This policy permits gays and lesbians to serve in the military provided they do not disclose their sexual orientation.[46] Additionally, military personnel are not permitted to inquire about a servicemember's sexual orientation. The law enacting this policy was passed in 1993 and has come under scrutiny by many civil rights groups. President Clinton intended to completely revoke the prohibition against gays and lesbians serving in the military but was met with strong opposition by many conservative and religious groups.[47]

Many people allege that the policy limits the enlistment of qualified people and requires the discharge of highly trained personnel who have publicly acknowledged their sexual orientation.[48] Since the policy took effect in 1994, more than 12,000 personnel have been discharged under it.[49] It has been estimated to cost the military $218 million to recruit and train replacements for those discharged under the policy.[50] Supporters of the policy allege that allowing gays and lesbians to serve openly in the military would drive away more people than would be discharged under the policy.[51] In July 2008, lawmakers held congressional hearings reexamining the policy for the first time since it came into law.[52]

PUBLIC OPINION DATA[53]

Currently, a majority of American respondents oppose allowing gays and lesbians to marry legally (65 percent in 1996 and 55 percent in

2007). However, a slight majority favor allowing civil unions for gay and lesbian couples (45 percent in 2003 and 54 percent in 2006). Additionally, a majority of respondents supports a constitutional amendment banning gay marriage (50 percent in 2003 and 2006, and 49 percent in 2008). When it comes to rights of gays and lesbians, a slight majority oppose allowing couples to adopt (57 percent in 1999 and 48 percent in 2006) and a plurality supports allowing gays and lesbians to openly serve in the military (41 percent in 2000 and 46 percent in 2007). Fifty-one percent of respondents indicated that if a presidential candidate was a strong supporter of gay rights, including same-sex marriages and gays and lesbians serving openly in the military, it would not make much difference in terms of their support of the candidate. Additionally, respondents would like to see homosexuality more widely accepted today (29 percent in 2001 and 34 percent in 2008).

When analyzed with earlier poll numbers, it appears that current attitudes toward gays and lesbians have evolved to become more positive and accepting. When Gallup first asked about the legality of homosexual relations in 1977, 43 percent favored the legalization of same-sex relationships.[54] Many years later in 2008, 55 percent favored it. Public opinion on the issue appeared to cement as the number of Americans reporting no opinion declined substantially to 5 percent in 2008 from 14 percent in 1977. Additionally, the 2003 *Lawrence v. Texas* Supreme Court decision that overturned state sodomy laws closely corresponded to Americans' increasing support for the legalization of homosexual relations. The lowest support for legalization, 32 percent, was reported in 1986.

Between 1977 and 2008, Americans were asked in polls, "Do you think homosexuals should or should not have equal rights in terms of job opportunities?" The data suggest that Americans have become more accepting of equal employment rights for gays and lesbians as the percentage of respondents who favored such rights increased from 56 percent in 1977 to 89 percent by 2008. It is interesting to note that although only a bare majority (52 percent) of Americans polled support the legalization of homosexual relations, more than eight in ten support equal job rights for gay men and lesbians.

Americans were also asked, "In your view, is homosexuality something a person is born with, or is homosexuality due to other factors such as upbringing and environment?" In June 1977, a majority (56 percent) of Americans polled thought that same-sex attraction was due to upbringing, 13 percent thought that a person was born gay, only 3 percent thought that same-sex attraction was caused by both factors, and 13 percent attributed it to neither factor. As recently as 1982, the majority of respondents (52 percent) still attributed same-sex attraction to upbringing or environment rather than biology. Although the number of respondents who believe that same-sex attraction is a biological trait has continued to rise, it still did not reach a majority by 2008.

Nevertheless, as of 2008, more Americans believed that a person is born homosexual rather than environment causing their sexual orientation (41 percent versus 38 percent).

Table 14.1: Do you favor or oppose the following? (In Percent)

United States		Favor	Oppose	Total (N)
Allowing gays and lesbians to marry legally				
	1996	27	65	92
				(1405)
	2007	36	55	91
				(1405)
Civil unions for gay couples				
	2003	45	47	92
				(1501)
	2006	54	42	96
				(1501)
Constitutional ban on gay marriage				
	2003	50	45	95
				(N/A)
	2006	50	47	97
				(N/A)
	2006	49	48	97
				(1501)
Adoption by gay couples				
	1999	38	57	95
				(1405)
	2006	46	48	94
				(1405)

Table 14.2: As you may know, under the current military policy, no one in the military is asked whether or not they are gay. But if they reveal that they are gay or they engage in homosexual activity, they will be discharged from the military. Do you personally think gays should be allowed to serve openly in the military, gays should be allowed to serve under the current policy, or gays should not be allowed to serve in the military under any circumstances?

		(In Percent)		
United States	Serve Openly	Serve under current policy	Not serve under any circumstances	No Opinion
2007	46	36	15	3
2000	41	38	17	4

Table 14.3: If you knew that a presidential candidate was a strong supporter of gay rights, including same-sex marriages and gays and lesbians serving openly in the military, would that make you more likely or less likely to vote for that candidate?

		(In Percent)			
United States	More Likely	Less Likely	Not Much Difference		Total (N)
2007	12	34	51	97	(1002)

Table 14.4: Would you like to see homosexuality be more widely accepted in this nation, less widely accepted, or is the acceptance of homosexuality in this nation today about right?

		(In Percent)			
United States	More widely accepted	Less widely accepted	About right	Other (vol.)	No opinion
2008	34	32	28	1	5
2007	33	37	27	*	3
2006	31	38	27	1	3
2005	29	36	30	1	4
2004	30	35	31	1	3
2003	28	31	34	1	6
2002	29	33	32	1	5
2001	29	34	33	1	3

*Less than 0.5%
(vol.)=Volunteered response

Table 14.5: Do you think homosexual relations between consenting adults should or should not be legal?

	(In Percent)		
United States	Should be legal	Should not be legal	No Opinion
2008	55	40	5
2007	59	37	4
2006^	56	40	4
2005	49	44	7
2004	46	49	5
2003	60	35	5
2002	52	43	5
2001	54	42	4
1999	50	43	7
1996	44	47	9
1992	48	44	8
1989	47	36	17
1988	35	57	11
1987	33	55	12
1986	33	54	13
1986	32	57	11
1985	44	47	9
1982	45	39	16
1977	43	43	14

^Asked of half sample

Table 14.6: As you may know, there has been considerable discussion in the news regarding the rights of homosexual men and women. In general, do you think homosexuals should or should not have equal rights in terms of job opportunities?

United States	Yes, should	No, should not	Depends (vol.)	No opinion
		(In Percent)		
2008	89	8	1	1
2007	89	8	1	2
2006^	89	9	1	1
2005	87	11	1	1
2004+	89	8	1	2
2003	88	10	1	1
2002	86	11	1	2
2001	85	11	3	1
1999	83	13	2	2
1996	84	12	2	2
1993	80	14	--	6
1992	74	18	--	8
1989	71	18	--	11
1982	59	28	--	13
1977	56	33	--	11

^Asked half sample
(vol.)=Volunteered response
+Wording: As you may know, there has been considerable discussion in the news regarding the rights of homo-sexual men and women. In general, do you think homosexuals should or should not have equal rights in terms of job opportunities?

Table 14.7: In your view, is homosexuality something a person is born with, or is homosexuality due to factors such as upbringing and environment?

United States	Born with	Upbringing/ environment	Both	Neither (vol.)	No opinion
		(In Percent)			
2008	41	38	9	2	9
2007	42	35	11	2	9
2006^	42	37	11	2	8
2005	38	44	10	2	6
2004	37	41	11	3	8
2003	38	44	11	2	5
2002	40	36	12	4	8
2001	40	39	9	3	9
1999	34	44	13	1	8
1996	31	40	13	3	13
1989	19	48	12	2	19
1982	17	52	13	2	16
1977	13	56	14	3	15

(vol.) = Volunteered response
^Asked of half sample

NOTES

1. D'Emilio, J. (1998). Sexual Politics, Sexual Communities: The Making of a Homosexual Minority in the United States, 1940–1970. Chicago: University of Chicago Press.

2. Ibid.

3. A Queer Notion of History, available at: http://chronicle.com/free/v50/i03/03a01401.htm (September 20, 2008).

4. Bauml Duberman, M. (1988). Reclaiming the gay past. *Reviews in American History* 16, pg 515–25.

5. Ibid. 515–25.

6. D'Emilio, J. (1998). Sexual Politics, Sexual Communities: The Making of a Homosexual Minority in the United States, 1940–1970. Chicago: University of Chicago Press.

7. A Queer Notion of History, available at: http://chronicle.com/free/v50/i03/03a01401.htm (September 20, 2008).

8. Ibid.

9. Ibid.

10. Bauml Dubermaln, M. (1988). Reclaiming the gay past. *Reviews in American History,* 16, pg. 515–25.

11. Ibid.

12. Facts about Homosexuality and Mental Health, available at: http://psychology.ucdavis.edu/rainbow/HTML/facts_mental_health.HTML (September 23, 2008).

13. "History of the Gay Rights Movement in the U.S.," http://www.lifeintheusa.com/people/gaypeople.htm (September 19, 2008).

14. D'Emilio, J. (1998). Sexual Politics, Sexual Communities: The Making of a Homosexual Minority in the United States, 1940–1970. Chicago: University of Chicago Press.

15. Infoplease, "The American Gay Rights Movement: A Timeline," available at: http://www.infoplease.com/ipa/A0761909.html (August 07, 2008).

16. Library of Congress, available at: http://thomas.loc.gov/cgi-bin/bdquery/z?d108:SJ00030:@@@L&summ2=m& (August 10, 2008).

17. Lectric Law Library, "Defense of Marriage Act," available at: http://www.lectlaw.com/files/leg23.htm (August 10, 2008).

18. Gay Law Net, available at: http://www.gaylawnet.com/ (August 5, 2008).

19. Fejes, F. (2008). *Gay rights and moral panic.* New York: Palgrave.

20. Ibid.

21. Ibid.

22. Infoplease, "The American Gay Rights Movement: A Timeline," available at: http://www.infoplease.com/ipa/A0761909.html (August 7, 2008).

23. Ibid.

24. Ibid.

25. Ibid.

26. Ibid.

27. Ibid.

28. National Conference of State Legislatures, "Same Sex Marriage," available at: http://www.ncsl.org/programs/cyf/samesex.htm (August 12, 2008).

29. Ibid.

30. "Calif. Supreme Court to take up gay marriage ban," available at: http://news.yahoo.com/s/ap/20081119/a-p_on_re_us/gay_marriage_lawsuits (December 14, 2008).

31. The Advocate, "oral Arguments on Prop. 8 begin March 5," available at: http://www.advocate.com/news_detail_ektid72346.asp (March 29, 2009.

32. Legal Information Institute, available at: http://www.law.cornell.edu/supct/html/historics/USSC_CR_0478_0186_ZS.html (August 10, 2008).

33. The U.S. Equal Employment Opportunity Commission, available at: http://www.eeoc.gov/federal/digest/xi-5-2.html (August 10, 2008).

34. Boy Scouts of America v. Dale, available at: http://law.jrank.org/pages/4831/Boy-Scouts-America-v-Dale.html (August 10, 2008).

35. Duke Law, "Lawrence v. Texas," available at: http://www.law.duke.edu/publiclaw/supremecourtonline/commentary/lawvtex.html (August 10, 2008).

36. Gay Law Net, available at: http://www.gaylawnet.com/ (August 05, 2008).

37. Ibid.

38. ACLU of Northern California, "Federal Appeals Court Says Schools Must Protect Gay Students from Harassment," available at: http://www.aclunc.org/news/press_releases/federal_appeals_court_says_schools_must_protect_gay_students_from_harassment.shtml (August 11, 2008).

39. National Gay and Lesbian Taskforce, available at: http://www.thetaskforce.org/downloads/reports/issue_maps/hate_crimes_04_08_color.pdf (August 5, 2008).

40. Gay Law Net, available at: http://www.gaylawnet.com/ (August 05, 2008).

41. Ibid.

42. Ibid.

43. Human Rights Watch, "The Uniting American Families Act," available at: http://www.hrw.org/campaigns/lgbt/uaf_act.htm (August 08, 2008).

44. "Leahy Introduces Bill to Provide equality under Immigration Law," available at: http://leahy.senate.gov/press/200902/021290b.html (March 29,2009).

45. National Public Radio, "Gay Refugees Seek Asylum in U.S.," available at: http://www.npr.org/templates/story/story.php?storyId=12734276 (August 12, 2008).

46. Los Angeles Times, "'Don't ask, don't tell' policy is reexamined," available at: http://www.latimes.com/news/printedition/asection/la-na-dontask24-2008jul24,0,1545463.story (August 10, 2008).

47. Infoplease, "The American Gay Rights Movement: A Timeline," available at: http://www.infoplease.com/ipa/A0761909.html (August 07, 2008).

48. Human Rights Watch, "Uniform Discrimination: The "Don't Ask,

Don't Tell" Policy of the U.S. Military," available at: http://www.hrw.org/ reports/2003/usa0103/ (August 02, 2008).

49. Ibid.

50. Ibid.

51. Ibid.

52. *Newsweek*, "Beginning the Conversation," available at: http://www. newsweek.com/id/147961 (August 12, 2008).

53. Data were obtained from the Pew Research Center for the People and the Press, the Pew Forum on Religion and Public Life, and Angus Reid, available at: http://www.angus-reid.com/polls/view/americans_want_ gays_to_serve_openly_in_military/, http://people-press.org/reports/display. php3?ReportID=273, http://pewforum.org/gay-marriage/ (August 11, 2008).

54. Information obtained from "America's changing attitudes toward homosexuality, civil unions, and same-gender marriage: 1977-2004," available at: http://findarticles.com/p/articles/mi_hb6467/is_1_52/ai_n29335755/pg_6 (December 12, 2008).

15

Argentina

Although Argentina does not federally permit civil unions, the city of Buenos Aires and the province of Río Negro grant them for same-sex couples.[1] Through these unions, couples are provided many benefits of marriage, including property rights, sick leave allowance for a partner's illness, and the sharing of social security services. Civil unions can be established for same-sex partners over the age of 21 who have lived in the province or city together for at least two years.[2] In 1997, legislation was passed allowing gays and lesbians to claim a widow or widower's pension. In 1998, a union-run health care program for teachers and flight attendants was extended to include health coverage for domestic partners.[3] In addition to allowing for civil unions, Buenos Aires also hosted the 2007 Gay World Cup of soccer and hosts the annual Gay Pride Parade.[4] Public opinion polls solidify the capital's mostly welcoming policies towards gays and lesbians, revealing that 73 percent of residents favor same-sex marriage (see table 16.1). Although Buenos Aires is now considered to be rather friendly towards gays and lesbians, the province prohibited gays and lesbians from voting until 1990.[5] An estimated 300 lesbians and gay men marched in Argentina's first Gay Pride Celebration that took place in Buenos Aires in 1992.[6]

In regards to other rights afforded gays and lesbians, Argentina does not give them special status in terms of immigration and does not grant asylum based on persecution for sexual orientation.[7] However, Argentina's military decriminalized homosexuality and lifted its ban on gay and lesbian participation in the military in February 2009.[8] In 2006, the Argentine Homosexual Community (CHA) received over 1,500 complaints of discrimination against gays and lesbians. Most of these complaints were regarding employment discrimination and

Table 15.1:   Do you agree or disagree with same-sex marriage?[*][1]

Argentina	Agree	Disagree	Total (N)
	(In percent)		
2006	73.1	25.6	100 (400)

*Respondents were only from the city of Buenos Aires.
[1] Data obtained from Angus Reid, available at: http://www.angus-reid.com/polls/view/urban_argentines_support_same_sex_marriage/ (June 17, 2008).

wrongful termination. Founded in 1984, the CHA is the longest running gay organization in Argentina.[9] The organization is involved in HIV/AIDS prevention and provides both legal and psychological counseling.[10] In addition, there have been reports of violence directed towards gays and lesbians.[11] There is no federal antidiscrimination law, but the cities of Rosario and Buenos Aires instituted their own bans on gay and lesbian discrimination.[12]

NOTES

1. Gay Law Net, available at: http://www.gaylawnet.com (June 17, 2008).
2. Ibid.
3. University of Minnesota, Human Rights Library, "international Recognition of Same-Sex Relationships," available at: http://hrlibrary.ngo.ru/eduman/hreduseries/TB3/act6/a6h3.htm (January 16, 2008).
4. *Los Angeles Times*, "Gay marriage reaction? It's all over the map," available at: http://www.latimes.com/news/local/la-me-worldwed17-2008jun17,0,3467680.story (June 17, 2008); Advocate.com, "Thousands march in gay pride parade in Argentine Capital," available at: http://www.advocate.com/news_detail_ektid50550.asp (June 25, 2008).
5. *"Con discriminación y represión no hay democracia"*: The lesbian and gay movement in Argentina, available at: http://bibliotecavirtual.clacso.org.ar/ar/libros/lasa97/brown.pdf (June 25, 2008).
6. "Queer Heritage," available at: http://www.aaronsgayinfo.com/timeline/Ftime90.html (December 8, 2008).
7. Partners Task Force, available at: http://buddybuddy.com/immigr.html (June 17, 2008).
8. *San Francisco Bay Times*, March 12, 2009, "Argentina Lifts Military Gay Ban," available at: http://www.sfbaytimes.com/?sex=article&article_id=10268 (March 27, 2009).
9. GAYBA, Comunidad Homosexual Argentina, available at: http://www.gay-ba.com (June 25, 2008).
10. Ibid.

11. U.S. Department of State, 2007 Country Reports on Human Rights Practices, Argentina, March 11, 2008, available at: http://www.state.gov/g/drl/rls/hrrpt/2007/100625.htm (June 17, 2008).

12. Gay Law Net, available at: http://www.gaylawnet.com (June 17, 2008).

⓰

Brazil

Brazil's policies on gay and lesbian rights vary depending upon the state and jurisdiction. Nationally, same-sex relationships are not legally recognized.[1] But some areas recognize relationships through domestic partnership laws. While not permitting same-sex marriages or civil unions, the Brazilian government recognizes same-sex partners as "de facto" partners, giving them legal status. This classification gives partners some of the same rights afforded to heterosexual, married couples.[2] The only state that permits same-sex civil unions is Rio Grande do Sul. Same-sex partners in that state can receive benefits such as the right to inherit partners' pensions and social security benefits, the ability to declare their partners as dependents on income tax returns, and additional rights related to child custody and insurance.[3] These rights did not come easily to the gay and lesbian community. In 1978, inspired by the international gay and lesbian movement, a group of gay writers and intellectuals began publishing a monthly journal entitled *Lampião da Esquina*. Based in Rio de Janeiro, *Lampião* served as a clearinghouse for the emerging politicized gay and lesbian movement. It also promoted the idea of building alliances with black groups, feminists, the indigenous movement, and ecologists. During its three-year run, *Lampião* solidified in Brazil the idea of coming out as a political act.[4] Sao Paulo and Rio de Janeiro police begin a yearlong investigation of *Lampião* on charges of offending public morality. With the support of the Brazilian journalists Union, activists fought the charges, and the case was dropped for lack of evidence.[5]

The state constitutions of Sergipe and Mato Grosso clearly prohibit discrimination based on sexual orientation. Many municipalities have also passed legislation banning such discrimination.[6] Although there are state and federal laws prohibiting discrimination based on sexual orientation, there have been reported instances of violence and abuse of gays and lesbians.[7] It was reported that 2,511 gays and lesbians were murdered between 1980 and 2005.[8] More recently, the NFO Bahian Gay Group reported that over 100 gays and lesbians were killed in 2007, identifying the northeast area of Brazil as the most violent.[9] Sao Paulo prohibits discrimination against homosexual, bisexual, or transgender citizens and Rio de Janeiro imposes fines as high as $5,500 against individuals or institutions found to discriminate against gays and lesbians.[10] Programs have been developed by nonprofit groups and nongovernmental organizations aimed at providing counseling, medical services, and a witness protection program to combat violence against gays and lesbians.[11] The "Brazil Without Homophobia" program promotes a message that a person's sexual orientation cannot be changed and encourages respect for diversity.[12] Since the program started, the Brazilian government has spent millions of dollars funding Gay Pride parades and pro–gay and lesbian TV programming and educational programs in schools.

Gays and lesbians who exhibit behavior which degrades military decorum and honor are barred from military service.[13] In addition, the Statute of the Military governs behavior expected by all personnel on and off duty.[14] An individual found guilty of engaging in libidinous acts, including homosexual acts, violates the penal code and is subject to punishment and possible discharge.[15] In June 2008, two Army sergeants were arrested after publicly admitting they are gay.[16] In 2003, the National Immigration Council began allowing visas to be given to same-sex partners of citizens who have legally formalized their relationship in Brazil or abroad. Couples must possess either a certification of concubinage, proof of a stable partnership, proof of mutual dependency, certification of cohabitation for at least five consecutive years, or proof of a common dependent child.[17]

PUBLIC OPINION DATA[18]

In a 2007 poll, 65 percent of respondents believed that homosexuality should be accepted and 30 percent believed that it should be rejected.[19] A minority of Brazilian respondents support allowing gays and lesbians to form civil unions (42 percent in 2006 and 39 percent in 2008).

Table 16.1: Do you support or oppose the following?

| Brazil | *(In Percent)* | | |
	Support	*Oppose*	*Total (N)*
Allowing same-sex couples to form civil unions			
2008	39	45	84
			(4044)
2006	42	49	91
			(4044)

NOTES

1. Human Rights Watch, available at: http://www.asylumlaw.org/docs/sexualminorities/HRWsamesexcouplesimmigration.pdf (July 17, 2008).

2. ReVista: Harvard Review of Latin America, available at: http://www.drclas.harvard.edu/revista/articles/view/967 (July 20, 2008).

3. Stonewall, available at: http://www.stonewall.org.uk/information_bank/partnership/international/137.asp#2 (July 18, 2008); The New York Times, "Brazil Grants Some Legal Recognition to Same-Sex Couples," available at: http://query.nytimes.com/gst/fullpage.html?res=9E04E4D71E3FF933A25755C0A9669C8B63 (July 20, 2008).

4. "Rio de Janeiro," available at: http://www.glbtq.com/social-sciences/rio_de_janeiro,2.html (December 8, 2008).

5. "Queer Heritage: A Timeline," available at: http://www.aaronsgayinfo.com/timeline/Ftime70.html (December 9, 2008).

6. Tønnesson, M., Andenæs, R., & Wintemute, M. A. (2001). *Legal Recognition of Same-Sex Partnerships*. Portland: Hart Publishing.

7. U.S. Department of State, 2007 Country Reports on Human Rights Practices, Brazil, March 11, 2008, available at: http://www.state.gov/g/drl/rls/hrrpt/2007/100630.htm (July 17, 2008).

8. IPS, available at: http://ipsnews.net/news.asp?idnews=37776 (July 18, 2008).

9. U.S. Department of State, 2007 Country Reports on Human Rights Practices, Brazil, March 11, 2008, available at: http://www.state.gov/g/drl/rls/hrrpt/2007/100630.htm (July 17, 2008).

10. Gay Law Net, available at: http://www.gaylawnet.com/ (July 20, 2008); The New York Times, "Brazil Grants Some Legal Recognition to Same-Sex Couples," available at: http://query.nytimes.com/gst/fullpage.html?res=9E04E4D71E3FF933A25755C0A9669C8B63 (July 20, 2008).

11. U.S. Department of State, 2007 Country Reports on Human Rights Practices, Brazil, March 11, 2008, available at: http://www.state.gov/g/drl/rls/hrrpt/2007/100630.htm (July 17, 2008).

12. LifeSiteNews.com, available at: http://www.lifesitenews.com/ldn/2007/jul/07073108.html (July 18, 2008).

13. United States General Accounting Office, "Homosexuals in the Military: Policies and Practices of Foreign Countries," available at: http://dont .stanford.edu/regulations/GAO.pdf (July 20, 2008).

14. Ibid.

15. Ibid.

16. Brazzil Magazine, "Public Admission of Being Gay Lands Brazilian Army Officers in Jail," available at: http://www.brazzilmag.com/content/ view/9393/1/ (July 20, 2008).

17. Human Rights Watch, available at: http://www.asylumlaw.org/docs/ sexualminorities/HRWsamesexcouplesimmigration.pdf (July 17, 2008).

18. Data obtained from Angus Reid Global Monitor, available at: http:// www.angus-reid.com/polls/view/many_still_oppose_same_sex_unions_in_ brazil/ (June 29, 2008).

19. Pew Global Attitudes Project, "World publics welcome global trade— but not Immigration," available at: http://pewglobal.org/reports/display .php?ReportID=258 (November 21, 2008).

⑰

Great Britain

Great Britain's history concerning its gay and lesbian population has changed throughout the years, with its foundation marked by the 1957 Wolfenden Report. This report recommended decriminalizing homosexual behavior between consenting adults.[1] In 1958 as a result of the Wolfenden Report, the Homosexual Law Reform Society (HLRS) was formed to lobby against laws criminalizing homosexuality.[2] Great Britain made civil partnerships legal in 2005 under the Civil Partnership Act. These partnerships allow same-sex couples to enjoy the same rights given to opposite-sex couples in marriage. Couples are given many legal rights, including next-of-kin privileges, employment and pensions benefits, protection from domestic violence, and recognition for immigration purposes.[3] In regards to immigration, sponsorship privileges have been available to unmarried couples of either sex since 1997 if the couple is in a committed relationship, have been living together for at least four years, intend to live together permanently, cannot legally marry in the United Kingdom, and one of them is present and lives in the United Kingdom.[4] This four year requirement has been criticized as being difficult to meet if one partner does not reside in the country or has restricted residency options due to a work or student visa.[5] The United Kingdom also considers applications for asylum based on a person's fear of persecution due to their sexual orientation.[6] In regards to military service, in the year 2000 Great Britain lifted its ban on allowing gays and lesbians to serve.[7] But it has been reported that the military remains hostile towards gays and lesbians.[8]

In the year 2000 with the Sexual Offences Amendment Act, the age of consent was set equal for both homosexual and heterosexual activity at 16 years of age.[9] In addition, this law changed a previous

Table 17.1: Do you absolutely agree, rather agree, rather disagree, or absolutely disagree with the following?

Great Britain	(In percent)				
	Absolutely Agree	Rather Agree	Rather Disagree	Absolutely Disagree	Total (N)
Authorization of homosexual marriages throughout Europe					
2003	17	30	15	30	92 (N/A)
2006		46*			N/A
Authorization of civil unions					
2004		65*	31~		N/A
Authorization of child adoption by homosexual couples throughout Europe					
2003	12	23	22	38	95 (N/A)
2006		33*			N/A
Authorization of adoption by lesbian couples					
1989		18*	78~		96 (N/A)
Authorization of adoption by gay male couples					
1989		10*	87~		97 (N/A)

*This percentage represents the total of people answering both "Absolutely Agree" and "Rather Agree."
~This percentage represents the total of people answering both "Absolutely Disagree" and "Rather Disagree."

provision and made sexual activity between two adult males legal provided no minors are present. Previously, the provision stated that such behavior was legal with no other people present.[10]

Although Great Britain has laws against discrimination based on sexual orientation, some incidents of violence have been reported. Great Britain's law encourages judges to impose harsher sentences in cases where sexual orientation is the basis for assaults. In addition, the police are providing their officers with specialized training in order to prevent these attacks.[11]

PUBLIC OPINION DATA[12]

In a 2007 poll, 71 percent of respondents believed that homosexuality should be accepted and 21 percent believed that it should be rejected.[13] A minority of British respondents approve of allowing gays and lesbians to marry legally (47 percent in 2003 and 46 percent in 2006). But the majority favors allowing same-sex couples to enter into civil unions (65 percent in 2004). When it comes to rights of gays and lesbians, a minority favors allowing couples to adopt (35 percent in 2003 and 33 percent in 2006). When broken down, more people favor allowing lesbian couples to adopt than gay male couples (18 percent and 10 percent, respectively, in 1989).

NOTES

1. BBC Home, available at: http://news.bbc.co.uk/onthisday/hi/dates/stories/september/4/newsid_3007000/3007686.stm (June 25, 2008).

2. British Library of Political and Economic Science, available at: http://www.aim25.ac.uk/cgi-bin/search2?coll_id=3213&inst_id=1 (June 25, 2008).

3. General Register Office, available at: http://www.gro.gov.uk/gro/content/civilpartnerships/ (May 30, 2008); Partners Task Force for Gay & Lesbian Couples, available at: http://buddybuddy.com/d-p-brit.html (May 30, 2008).

4. Center for Immigration Studies, available at: http://www.cis.org/articles/1999/back599.html (May 30, 2008).

5. Partners Task Force for Gay & Lesbian Couples, available at: http://buddybuddy.com/immigr.html (May 30, 2008).

6. Ibid.

7. Glbtq, "Military Culture: European," available at: http://www.glbtq.com/social-sciences/military_culture_eur.html (May 30, 2008).

8. Ibid.

9. Partners Task Force for Gay & Lesbian Couples, available at: http://buddybuddy.com/immigr.html (May 30, 2008).

10. Ibid.

11. U.S. Department of State, 2007 Country Reports on Human Rights Practices, United Kingdom, March 11, 2008, available at: http://www.state.gov/g/drl/rls/hrrpt/2007/100591.htm (May 30, 2008).

12. Data were obtained from Gallup Europe, available at: http://www.ilga-europe.org/europe/issues/marriage_and_partnership/public_opinion_and_same_sex_unions_2003 (May 28, 2008); Gallup, available at: http://www.gallup.com/poll/13561/Gay-Rights-US-More-Conservative-Than-Britain-Canada.aspx (May 30, 2008); Brook, L., et al. (1992). *British social attitudes cumulative sourcebook.* London: Gower; Jowell, R., et al. (1991). In *British social attitudes: The 8th report.* London: Dartmouth.

13. Pew Global Attitudes Project, "World publics welcome global trade—but not Immigration," available at: http://pewglobal.org/reports/display.php?ReportID=258 (November 21, 2008).

18

France

France has a unique way of recognizing same-sex partners and granting them some of the legal rights of marriage. Instituted in 1999 and called a Civil Solidarity Pact (PACS), both heterosexual and homosexual couples may sign an agreement and receive legal recognition of their relationships.[1] Before the existence of PACS, unmarried couples in France had no legal status. When a couple signs a PACS, they are entitled to several benefits. A person who has not jointly signed a lease with the other is entitled to have the lease transferred to him or her from the other partner.[2] Rights to take leave from work and authorizations of absence for family reasons are extended to couples who sign a PACS, as well as some social welfare benefits.[3] In addition, the signing of a PACS is taken into consideration in public service job postings and applications for permanent resident status. Partners are taxed jointly three years after signing a PACS. Since PACS have existed, approximately 75,000 have signed one.[4] While the existence of PACS has helped the gay and lesbian community achieve legal recognition in partnerships, PACS have been criticized for not affording same-sex partners the same rights given to heterosexual partners. Under PACS, unmarried couples must wait three years before filing jointly on their taxes, do not receive the same consideration under immigration law, and cannot adopt children.[5] Regarding immigration, one must prove he or she has an independent means of support for one year on a tourist visa before applying for permanent resident status.[6]

Besides the existence of PACS, France has also made strides to eliminate discrimination against gays and lesbians. In 1982, the law governing age of consent for homosexual activity was lowered from

18 to 15 to match the age of consent for heterosexual activity. Before this change, legislation on civil servants and tenants that mandated good, moral conduct was inherently discriminating against gays and lesbians.[7] France was the first country to legislate gay and lesbian rights in 1985 by amending the penal code to prohibit discrimination on the grounds of "moral habits" which included sexual orientation.[8] In 2004, France enacted a law making homophobic and sexist remarks illegal. Christian Vanneste was the first person to be prosecuted under this law in 2006.[9] France also has laws prohibiting discrimination on the basis of sexual orientation in the workforce[10] and allows gays and lesbians to serve in the military.[11]

PUBLIC OPINION DATA[12]

In a 2007 poll, 83 percent of respondents believed that homosexuality should be accepted and 17 percent believed that it should be rejected.[13] A majority and near majority of French respondents approve of allowing gays and lesbians to marry legally (58 percent in 2003 and 48 percent in 2006). But only a minority favor allowing gay and lesbian couples to adopt (39 percent in 2003 and 35 percent in 2006). Over the past 20 years, the French have come to view homosexuality less as a disease that needs to be cured (42 percent in 1973 and 23 percent in 1997) and more as an acceptable lifestyle (24 percent in 1973 and 55 percent in 2006).

Table 18.1: Do you absolutely agree, rather agree, rather disagree, or absolutely disagree with the following?

France		(In percent)				
		Absolutely Agree	Rather Agree	Rather Disagree	Absolutely Disagree	Total (N)
Authorization of homosexual marriages throughout Europe						
	2003	25	33	14	26	98 (N/A)
	2006		48*			N/A
Authorization of child adoption by homosexual couples throughout Europe						
	2003	12	27	22	38	99 (N/A)
	2006		35*			N/A

*This percentage represents the total of people answering both "Absolutely Agree" and "Rather Agree."

Table 18.2:   What is your view of homosexuality?

	(In Percent)				
	L'Express poll December 1973	Elle poll January 1981	GI poll December 1987	Le Nouvel Observateur poll October 1987	Le Nouvel Observateur poll June 1997
A disease which has to be cured	42	34	28	27	23
A sexual perversion which has to be fought against	22	24	19	24	17
An acceptable lifestyle	24	29	41	36	55
No opinion	12	13	12	13	5

NOTES

1. Embassy of France in the U.S., available at: http://www.ambafrance-us.org/atoz/pacs.asp (May 20, 2008).

2. Ibid.

3. Ibid.

4. Ibid.

5. Ibid.

6. Immigration Roundup, available at: http://www.buddybuddy.com/immigr.html (May 20, 2008).

7. *Homophobia, Vichy France, and the "Crime of Homosexuality": The Origins of the Ordinance of 6 August 1942,* GLQ: A Journal of Lesbian and Gay Studies - Volume 8, Number 3, 2002, pp. 301–318.

8. Queer Heritage, Gay Historical Timeline, available at: http://www.aaronsgayinfo.com/timeline/time80.html (June 25, 2008).

9. LifeSite News, available at: http://www.lifesitenews.com/ldn/2006/jan/06012609.html (May 20, 2008).

10. U.S. Department of State, 2007 Country Reports on Human Rights Practices, France, March 11, 2008, available at: http://www.state.gov/g/drl/rls/hrrpt/2007/100559.htm (May 20, 2008).

11. Human Rights Watch, available at: http://www.hrw.org/wr2k1/special/gay.html (May 20, 2008).

12. Data obtained from France Queer Resources Directory, available at: http://www.france.qrd.org/texts/partnership/fr/explanation.html (May 20, 2008); Embassy of France in the U.S., available at: http://www.ambafrance-us.org/atoz/pacs.asp (May 20, 2008).

13. Pew Global Attitudes Project, "World publics welcome global trade—but not Immigration," available at: http://pewglobal.org/reports/display.php?ReportID=258 (November 21, 2008).

Germany

Although not recognizing same-sex marriages, in 2001 Germany began to allow registered partnerships for same-sex couples that give them the same sets of responsibilities as marriage and some of the same rights.[1] Partners are still taxed singly and subject to different exemption amounts in inheritance tax. In 2004, revisions to the act extended more rights to same-sex partners. These rights include the ability of partners to adopt the other's children, extension of pension rights, and simpler divorce rules.[2] Estimates of the number of registered partnerships in 2004 were over 6,000.[3] But the same tax rules apply and partners do not have the right to adopt jointly. In addition, same-sex partners are allowed to take the other's last name.[4]

Homosexuality was decriminalized in 1968 in East Germany and in 1969 in West Germany.[5] In regards to immigration, Germany grants applications for asylum to gays and lesbians.[6] In addition, Germany allows gays and lesbians to serve openly in the military.[7] In 2006, Germany enacted a law prohibiting general discrimination on the basis of sexual orientation.[8] Although Germany is making strides to provide gays and lesbians with greater equality in society, there have been some reports of discrimination in the workplace and in society.[9] In a 2007 poll, 81 percent of respondents believed that homosexuality should be accepted and 17 percent believed that it should be rejected.[10]

The Lifetime Partnership Act also provided equal immigration rights to same-sex couples. Partners of German citizens can apply for visas if they show their partner is sponsoring them and they have the intention of registering their partnership once in the country.[11] Temporary residents already in Germany can become permanent residents when their partnership is registered.[12] The sponsoring partners must show that he or she is able to financially support both partners and that he or she is not receiving social assistance.[13]

NOTES

1. Gaylawnet, available at: http://www.gaylawnet.com (June 10, 2008).
2. Ibid.
3. Global Gayz, available at: http://www.globalgayz.com/german-news03 -06.html#article11 (June 10, 2008).
4. Ibid.
5. Ibid.
6. Ibid.
7. Tom Head, "Lesbians and Gay Men in the Military," available at: http://civilliberty.about.com/od/gendersexuality/ig/Lesbian-and-Gay-Rights -101/Gays-in-the-Military.htm (June 10, 2008).
8. U.S. Department of State, 2007 Country Reports on Human Rights Practices, Germany, March 11, 2008, available at: http://www.state.gov/g/drl/ rls/hrrpt/2007/100561.htm (June 9, 2008).
9. Ibid.
10. Pew Global Attitudes Project, "World publics welcome global trade— but not Immigration," available at: http://pewglobal.org/reports/display .php?ReportID=258 (November 21, 2008).
11. Human Rights Watch, available at: http://www.asylumlaw.org/docs/ sexualminorities/HRWsamesexcouplesimmigration.pdf (June 10, 2008).
12. Ibid.
13. Ibid.

⓴

Italy

Italy is in the majority of countries that offer neither marriage privileges nor civil union recognition to same-sex couples.[1] While these policies are not instituted on a federal basis, some cities have taken steps towards recognizing same-sex relationships. The Valle d'Aosta region provides some rights to same-sex couples such as the ability to take out a loan together.[2] The cities of Bologna, Florence, Pisa, Ferrara, and Terni have instituted civil registers that, while being mainly symbolic and having no legal implications, take note of same-sex partnerships.[3] The Pisa City Council offers a discount on loan mortgages to couples who are in a committed relationship, under thirty-five years of age, and have a modest income.[4] A priest in the city of Pinerolo was given an order to leave the priesthood after performing several gay marriage ceremonies in his church.[5]

The gay and lesbian community has been afforded some legal protection in regard to discrimination. The Statute Commission of the Regional Council of Tuscany instituted a statute making it unlawful to discriminate based on characteristics such as gender, age, religion, and sexual tendency.[6] Also, consensual sex between same-sex couples is legal under Italy's criminal law.[7] Italy has no official policy on allowing gays into the military but allows gay men to be exempted from the mandatory military service requirement if they say they fear discrimination based on their homosexuality.[8] There have been reports, however, that overt homosexual behavior has been grounds for dismissal from the military.

In addition to Italy's protections, there are several European Union laws that offer protection from discrimination based on sexual orientation. The European Parliament passed many nonbinding resolutions that called for an end to work-related discrimination based on sexual orientation.[9] The Parliament also passed a resolution saying that it would not give its consent for the inclusion of countries into the European Union that violate the rights of gays and lesbians through their policies or legislation.[10]

There have been reports, however, of discrimination based on sexual orientation by Italians. In 2007, a student in Sicily was abused by his classmates and expelled from school because he was believed to be gay.[11] In 2005, the Ministry of Transport requested the revocation of a man's driver's license due to his sexual orientation. Both cases were investigated and the latter ended in a civil suit.[12] Many gay and lesbian rights organizations have formed to counter this discrimination. The most well-known group is Arcigay, founded in 1985. It works to "combat homophobia, heterosexism, prejudice and anti-gay discrimination. It is committed to achieving equal status and equal opportunities among all individuals regardless of sexual orientation, and aims to reinforce a full, free and happy life for gay people."[13]

PUBLIC OPINION DATA[14]

In a 2007 poll, 65 percent of respondents believed that homosexuality should be accepted and 23 percent believed that it should be rejected.[15]

Table 20.1:   Do you absolutely agree, rather agree, rather disagree, or absolutely disagree with the following?

Italy	(In percent)				
	Absolutely Agree	Rather Agree	Rather Disagree	Absolutely Disagree	Total (N)
Authorization of homosexual marriages throughout Europe					
2003	17	30	15	37	99 (N/A)
2006		31*			N/A
Authorization of child adoption by homosexual couples throughout Europe					
2003	9	16	24	50	99 (N/A)
2006		24*			N/A
Italy's civil partnership law					
2007		45*	47*		92 (1917)

*This percentage represents the total of people answering both "Absolutely Agree" and "Rather Agree."

A minority of Italian respondents approve of allowing gays and lesbians to marry legally (47 percent in 2003 and 31 percent in 2006). When it comes to rights of gays and lesbians, a minority favor allowing couples to adopt (25 percent in 2003 and 24 percent in 2006). In addition, a slight majority do not favor Italy having a civil partnership law (47 percent in 2007).

NOTES

1. Gay Law Net, available at: http://www.gaylawnet.com/ (May 22, 2008).
2. Ibid.
3. Ibid.
4. Ibid.
5. Ibid.
6. Ibid.
7. Ibid.
8. Ibid.
9. Human Rights Education Associates, available at: http://www.hrea.org (May 22, 2008).
10. Ibid.
11. U.S. Department of State, 2007 Country Reports on Human Rights Practices, Italy, March 11, 2008, available at: http://www.state.gov/g/drl/rls/hrrpt/2007/100566.htm (May 22, 2008).
12. Ibid.
13. Arcigay, available at: http://www.arcigay.it/arcigay-english (June 29, 2008).
14. Data were obtained from the Pew Research Center for the People and the Press and the Pew Forum on Religion and Public Life. See "Less Opposition to Gay Marriage, Adoption and Military Service" and "Gay Marriage" available at http://people-press.org/reports/display.php3?ReportID=273 and http://pewforum.org/gay-marriage/; Angus Reid Global Monitor, available at http://www.angus-reid.com/polls/view/italians_divided_over_civil_partnership_law/ (June 29, 2008)
15. Pew Global Attitudes Project, "World publics welcome global trade—but not Immigration," available at: http://pewglobal.org/reports/display.php?ReportID=258 (November 21, 2008).

㉑

Sweden

On April 2, 2009, the *Washington Post* reported that "The Swedish Parliament adopted a law that gives same-sex couples the same marriage rights as those enjoyed by heterosexuals. The Parliament's website says the law will take effect May 1."[1]

Sweden is one of the more involved countries when it comes to gay and lesbian rights and has established many policies that support that ideal. While Sweden does not allow same-sex couples to marry, couples are able to be recognized through registered partnerships that grant them the same benefits provided to heterosexual couples in marriage.[2] This law was enacted in 1994 and also allows for registered partners to adopt jointly. Previously, a single parent could adopt a child after passing a battery of tests and if there was another person of the opposite sex willing to commit to providing a gender role model for the child.[3] Additionally, in 2005 in-vitro fertilization was allowed for lesbian couples.[4] There has been some controversy over the fact that the separation rate for gay and lesbian couples is much higher than the rate for married heterosexual couples (30 percent of lesbians, 20 percent of gays; 13 percent of opposite-sex couples).[5] As an alternative to registered partnerships, a 2003 Swedish law grants limited rights, mostly concerning property, to unregistered couples of either sex.[6]

In regards to Swedish law, homosexual activity was legalized in 1944 and the age of consent was set at fifteen in 1978 (regardless of sexual orientation). Homosexuality has not been considered a disease since 1979.[7] In 1987, the Swedish Penal Code was altered to include a law banning discrimination on the basis of sexual orientation.[8] In addition, Sweden's criminal law concerning sex crimes is written in gender-neutral language and does not distinguish between sexual orientation.[9] Furthermore, gays and lesbians are permitted to serve in the military.[10] Sweden also grants asylum based on a person's fear of persecution over his or her sexual orientation.[11] In regards to immigration, Sweden grants immigration privileges to same-sex couples, allowing one person who is already a citizen to sponsor his or her partner for citizenship.[12] While Sweden is generally accepting of gays and lesbians, there have been a small number of reported acts of violence and discrimination. There were 45 reported cases in 2006 and 47 cases in 2007 of discrimination based on sexual orientation and 8 new discrimination investigations were started in 2007, compared with 11 investigations in 2006.[13]

PUBLIC OPINION DATA[14]

In a 2007 poll, 86 percent of respondents believed that homosexuality should be accepted and only 9 percent believed that it should be rejected.[15] A majority of Swedish respondents approve of allowing gays and lesbians to marry legally (69 percent in 2003 and 71 percent in 2006). When it comes to rights of gays and lesbians, the population is fairly split on allowing couples to adopt (43 percent in 2003 and 51 percent in 2006).

Table 21. 1: **Do you absolutely agree, rather agree, rather disagree, or absolutely disagree with the following?**

Sweden	(In percent)				
	Absolutely Agree	Rather Agree	Rather Disagree	Absolutely Disagree	Total (N)
Authorization of homosexual marriages throughout Europe					
2003	51	18	5	21	95 (N/A)
2006		71*			N/A
2008		71*	24*		95 (1000)
Authorization of child adoption by homosexual couples throughout Europe					
2003	27	16	12	38	93 (N/A)
2006		51*			N/A

*This percentage represents the total of people answering both "absolutely agree" and "rather agree."

NOTES

1. *Washington Post*, April 2, 2009, p. A13.
2. Gay Law Net, available at: http://www.gaylawnet.com/ (May 28, 2008).
3. Ibid.
4. Ibid.
5. Ibid.
6. Ibid.
7. Swedish Institute, available at: http://www.historia.su.se/personal/jens_rydstrom/artiklar/ombudsman_e.pdf (June 29, 2008).
8. Ibid.
9. Swedish Institute, available at: http://www2.historia.su.se/personal/jens_rydstrom/artiklar/ombudsman_e.pdf (May 28, 2008); Chapter 6 of the Swedish Penal Code 1962:700, available at: http://www.sweden.gov.se/sb/d/574/a/47455 (May 28, 2008).
10. Homosexuals in the military: Policies and practices of foreign countries, available at: http://dont.stanford.edu/regulations/GAO.pdf (May 28, 2008).
11. Opening the Doors of Immigration: Sexual Orientation and Asylum in the United States, available at: http://www.wcl.american.edu/hrbrief/v6i3/immigration.htm (May 28, 2008).
12. Homosexuals and Immigration Developments in the United States and Abroad, available at: http://www.cis.org/articles/1999/back599.html (May 28, 2008).
13. U.S. Department of State, 2007 Country Reports on Human Rights Practices, Russia, March 11, 2008, available at: http://www.state.gov/g/drl/rls/hrrpt/2007/100581.htm (June 29, 2008).
14. Data obtained from Gallup Europe, available at: http://www.ilga-europe.org/europe/issues/marriage_and_partnership/public_opinion_and_same_sex_unions_2003 (May 28, 2008) and Angus Reid Global Monitor, available at: http://www.angus-reid.com/polls/view/swedes_support_same_sex_marriage/ (June 29, 2008)
15. Pew Global Attitudes Project, "World publics welcome global trade—but not Immigration," available at: http://pewglobal.org/reports/display.php?ReportID=258 (November 21, 2008).

Hungary

In 2007, the Hungarian government approved making registered partnerships available to both same-sex and opposite-sex couples. These partnerships, which were supposed to begin being issued on January 1, 2009, would have given couples many of the same protections and rights of marriage. However, in December 2008, Hungary's Constitution Court struck down the law as unconstitutional. The Registered Partnership Act gave both gay and heterosexual couples the right to register their partnership and protections regarding next of kin status, taxation, health care, inheritance, social security, pensions, and shared possession of a home.[1] The Court found that creating an institution similar to marriage for both same sex and opposite sex couples duplicates the institution of marriage for opposite sex couples, and therefore contradicts the special protection of marriage given in the Constitution.[2] However, the Court also ruled that same-sex couples have the right to an institution similar to marriage and Prime Minister Ferenc Gyurcsany instructed the Minister of Justice and Law Enforcement to prepare a new bill on registered partnerships taking into account the opinion of the Court. The new bill was approved by the government in February 2009 and retains much of the content of the previous bill with one exception: registered partnerships would only be available to same-sex couples. Establishment and dissolution of registered partnerships would be the same as for marriage, and registered partners would be entitled to most of the rights available for married couples. Notable exceptions are the right to take the partner's name and the right to adopt children.[3] Besides introducing registered partnerships for same-sex couples, the bill would also introduce a new system for registering domestic partnerships. Unlike registered partnerships, domestic partnerships would not grant any new rights or duties to unmarried, cohabiting couples, but would make it easier for them to prove the existence of their relationships.[4] As of March 2009, the bill had not yet been adopted by the Parliament.

Currently, same-sex couples can receive some rights of marriage through common-law marriages. Common-law marriage applications are managed by the social department of the local government and benefits are awarded on a case-by-case basis to couples living together in an economic and sexual relationship.[5] Separate from common-law marriages, gays and lesbians are able to inherit property and receive pensions from their deceased partners.[6] In addition to these rights given to same-sex couples, gays and lesbians are able to serve in the military but are not afforded privileges related to immigration and asylum.[7]

In terms of Hungary's laws, homosexuality was decriminalized in 1961 and consensual sex between same-sex couples is legal.[8] Additionally, laws banning discrimination on the basis of sexual orientation were introduced in 2003. Without these laws, there would be no legislation protecting gays and lesbians from such discrimination.[9] In 2002, the Hungarian Constitutional Court repealed a paragraph in the penal code that had set the age of consent for heterosexual activity at 14 and homosexual activity at 18. The age of consent was set at fourteen regardless of sexual orientation.[10]

While homosexuality is legal in Hungary, there have been some instances of discrimination. In 2007, there was public outcry over the police's lack of protection of participants in a lesbian, gay, bisexual, and transgender (LGBT) march. People alleged that the police failed to adequately contend with counterdemonstrators that became violent towards the march's participants and failed to come to the assistance of many people who felt threatened and requested police protection.[11] Several NGOs criticized the police's inaction and their decision to charge people with group disorderly conduct instead of the more serious charge of incitement against a community or violation of the freedom of assembly.[12]

PUBLIC OPINION DATA[13]

A minority of Hungarian respondents approve of allowing gays and lesbians to marry legally (37 percent in 2003 and 18 percent in 2006). When it comes to rights of gays and lesbians, a minority favor allowing couples to adopt (34 percent in 2003 and 13 percent in 2006).

Table 22.1: Do you absolutely agree, rather agree, rather disagree, or absolutely disagree with the following?

Hungary	(In percent)				
	Absolutely Agree	Rather Agree	Rather Disagree	Absolutely Disagree	Total (N)
Authorization of homosexual marriages throughout Europe					
2003	14	23	12	43	92 (N/A)
2006		18*			N/A
Authorization of child adoption by homosexual couples throughout Europe					
2003	13	21	14	47	95 (N/A)
2006		13*			N/A

*This percentage represents the total of people answering both "absolutely agree" and "rather agree."

NOTES

1. "Hungarian Government Proposes Registered Same-Sex Partnerships," Pink News. Available at: http://www.pinknews.co.uk/news/articles/2005-11133.html (March 27.2009).

2. Ibid.

3. Ibid.

4. Ibid.

5. Ibid.

6. Ibid.

7. Ibid.

8. Ibid.

9. Ibid.

10. ILGA Europe, available at: http://www.france.qrd.org/assocs/ilga/euroletter/101.html (June 2, 2008).

11. ILGA, Participants of pride march attached in Hungary, available at: http://www.ilga-europe.org/europe/guide/country_by_country/hungary/participants_of_pride_march_attacked_in_hungary (June 2, 2008).

12. U.S. Department of State, 2006 Country Reports on Human Rights Practices, Hungary, March 6, 2007, available at: http://www.state.gov/g/drl/rls/hrrpt/2007/100563.htm (June 2, 2008).

13. Data obtained from Gallup Europe, see http://www.ilga-europe.org/europe/issues/marriage_and_partnership/public_opinion_and_same_sex_unions_2003 (June 2, 2008).

Poland

Poland has experienced a large amount of conflict with its gay and lesbian community, mainly due to its large Roman Catholic community that has made its anti-gay stance very public.[1] Poland does not provide for legal recognition of same-sex couples; in fact, Poland's Constitution expressly describes marriage as a "union of a man and a woman."[2] But in 2003 Senator Maria Szyszkowska proposed civil unions for same-sex couples called registered partnerships which, if it had passed, would have resembled France's PACS.[3] Also in 2003 Poland's Labour Code was amended to include antidiscrimination provisions.[4] Although the Constitution prohibits discrimination for any reason, it does not specifically mention sexual orientation.[5]

In 1948, the age of consent for both heterosexual and homosexual sexual activity was set at 15.[6] Poland offers limited rights to its gay and lesbian citizens, bans adoption by same sex couples and allows no special provisions related to immigration and asylum.[7] Poland does allow gays and lesbians to openly serve in the military but they may be discharged or denied promotions under limited circumstances.[8]

Poland is dealing with a large amount of discrimination and violence directed toward its gay and lesbian population. Counter marches were organized in protest of Krakow's annual gay March for Tolerance in 2007, resulting in several arrests due to disorderly conduct.[9] Also in 2007, the Minister of Education called homosexuality immoral and denounced the annual Equality Parade.[10] Additionally, the UN Committee Against Torture (CAT) recommended that the Polish government make hate crimes motivated by sexual orientation a criminal offense due to its concerns over pervasive violence and intolerance.[11]

Table 23. 1:   Do you absolutely agree, rather agree, rather disagree, or absolutely
disagree with the following?

	(In percent)				
Poland	Absolutely Agree	Rather Agree	Rather Disagree	Absolutely Disagree	Total (N)
Authorization of homosexual marriages throughout Europe					
2003	7	11	14	56	88 (N/A)
2006		17*			N/A
Authorization of child adoption by homosexual couples throughout Europe					
2003	3	7	12	63	85 (N/A)
2006		7*			N/A

*This percentage represents the total of people answering both "absolutely agree" and "rather agree."

PUBLIC OPINION DATA[12]

In a 2007 poll, 45 percent of respondents believed that homosexuality should be accepted and 41 percent believed that it should be rejected.[13] A small minority of Polish respondents approve of allowing gays and lesbians to marry legally (18 percent in 2003 and 17 percent in 2006). When it comes to rights of gays and lesbians, a small minority favor allowing couples to adopt (10 percent in 2003 and 7 percent in 2006). These are extremely low numbers in comparison to other European countries, which partly resulted in Poland's listing as one of the world's worst countries to live in for a gay or lesbian person.[14] Poland ranks number eight after Uganda, Iran, Egypt, Saudi Arabia, Nigeria, United Arab Emirates, and Cameroon and before Nepal and India.[15]

NOTES

1. Glbtq, available at: http://www.glbtq.com/social-sciences/poland.html (June 10, 2008).

2. Polish Constitution, Article 18, available at: http://www.servat.unibe .ch/icl/pl00000_.html (June 10, 2008).

3. International Gay and Lesbian Human Rights Commission, available at: http://www.iglhrc.org/site/iglhrc/content.php?type=1&id=91 (June 10, 2008).

4. European Industrial Relations Observatory On-Line, available at: http://www.eurofound.europa.eu/eiro/2003/11/feature/pl0311108f.htm (June 10, 2008).

5. Glbtq, available at: http://www.glbtq.com/social-sciences/poland.html (June 10, 2008); Polish Constitution, Article 32, available at: http://www.servat.unibe.ch/icl/pl00000_.html (June 10, 2008).

6. Ibid.

7. Queertry, available at: http://www.queerty.com/poland-rejects-eus-gay-adoption-ruling-20080123/; Partners Task Force for Gay & Lesbian Couples, available at: http://www.buddybuddy.com/immigr.html (June 10, 2008).

8. Human Rights Watch, available at: http://www.hrw.org/reports/2003/usa0103/USA0103FINAL-09.htm (June 10, 2008).

9. U.S. Department of State, 2007 Country Reports on Human Rights Practices, Poland, March 11, 2008, available at: http://www.state.gov/g/drl/rls/hrrpt/2007/100578.htm (June 9, 2008).

10. Ibid.

11. Ibid.

12. Data obtained from Gallup Europe, see http://www.ilga-europe.org/europe/issues/marriage_and_partnership/public_opinion_and_same_sex_unions_2003 (June 9, 2008).

13. Pew Global Attitudes Project, "World publics welcome global trade—but not Immigration," available at: http://pewglobal.org/reports/display.php?ReportID=258 (November 21, 2008).

14. Southern Voice, available at: http://www.southernvoice.com/2006/3-17/news/national/abuse.cfm (June 10, 2008).

15. Ibid.

Russia

Russia's policies regarding gays and lesbians have evolved since the fall of the Soviet Union. The clause of the Criminal Code that criminalized sex between men in 1933 was repealed in 1993. Before 1993, same-sex acts were punishable by prison terms of up to five years.[1] Although homosexuality is not illegal, Russia does not recognize same-sex marriage. Although homosexuality is not illegal, Russia does not recognize same sex marriage and gay and lesbian couples are unable to jointly adopt children. Gays and lesbians are also not afforded asylum due to discrimination based on their sexual orientation and couples are not given special immigration privileges.[2]

Russia's policy on allowing gays and lesbians to serve in the military is unique. Gays and lesbians who have problems or are uncomfortable with their sexual orientation are allowed to be drafted only in times of war.[3] Gay activists believe that this policy allows well-adjusted gay and lesbians to serve in the military.[4] However, under health screening requirements, people who are HIV positive are not allowed to serve.[5]

Although homosexuality is legal, Russia has experienced some issues with discrimination directed towards gays and lesbians. Gays and lesbians have experienced problems receiving healthcare services, obtaining employment, and have been subject to police discrimination. The employment discrimination occurs even though the St. Petersburg court ruled in 2005 that it is illegal for an employer to discriminate against a man based on his sexual orientation.[6] In 2006, demonstrators in a Moscow gay rights march were not adequately protected by the police during assaults by counterdemonstrators.[7] Police have often been accused of failing to protect gay and lesbian protestors. In 2008, the mayor of Moscow banned gay events in the city under harsh criticism from activists.[8]

PUBLIC OPINION DATA[9]

In a 2007 poll, 20 percent of respondents believed that homosexuality should be accepted and 64 percent believed that it should be rejected.[10]

A majority of Russian respondents disapprove of allowing gays and lesbians to marry legally (59 percent in 2005). If the candidate that a respondent liked for the president of Russia announced his homosexuality, a small minority of respondents would still vote for the candidate (13 percent in 2005). In addition, many people favor prosecution of homosexual relations between consenting adults even though it is not illegal (43 percent in 2005).

Table 24.1: Do you agree or disagree with homosexual couples having the right to marry?

Russia	Completely Agree	Somewhat Agree	Partly Agree/ Disagree	Somewhat Disagree	Completely Disagree	Total (N)
			(In Percent)			
2005	4	10	17	25	34	90 (1600)

Table 24.2: If before the elections of the President of Russia, the candidate you like announced his homosexuality, you will most likely:

Russia	Still Vote for Candidate	Vote for another Candidate	Vote Against All/Not Vote	Total (N)
		(In Percent)		
2005	13	43	21	77 (1600)

Table 24.3: Do you think homosexual relations between consenting adults should or should not be prosecuted in Russia?

Russia	Should be Prosecuted	Should Not be Prosecuted	Total (N)
2005	43	38	81 (1600)

NOTES

1. Gay Rights in Russia and Russian Gay Life, available at: http://gaylife .about.com/od/world/a/russian.htm (June 29, 2008).

2. Partners Task Force for Gay and Lesbian Couples, available at: http:// www.buddybuddy.com/immigr.html (June 29, 2008).

3. Glbtq, available at: http://www.glbtq.com/social-sciences/military_ culture_eur.html (June 29, 2008).

4. Ibid.

5. Gay Law Net, available at: http://www.gaylawnet.com/ (June 29, 2008).

6. Ibid.

7. U.S. Department of State, 2007 Country Reports on Human Rights Practices, Russia, March 11, 2008, available at: http://www.state.gov/g/drl/rls/ hrrpt/2007/100581.htm (June 29, 2008).

8. Russia News & Reports, available at: http://www.globalgayz.com/ russia-news04-05.html (June 29, 2008).

9. Data obtained from Angus Reid Global Monitor, available at: http:// www.angus-reid.com/polls/view/5986 (June 29, 2008) and Levada Centre, available at: http://www.GayRussia.ru (June 29, 2008).

10. Pew Global Attitudes Project, "World publics welcome global trade— but not Immigration," available at: http://peewglobal.org/reports/display .php?ReportID=258 (November 21, 2008).

25

Israel

Israel's policies towards gays and lesbians are liberal in relation to other countries in the Middle East. For example, homosexuality is legal between consenting adults and there is no legal discrimination against gays and lesbians.[1] The Israeli Parliament decriminalized sex acts between consenting adults of the same sex in 1988 and lowered the age of consent for homosexual activity from 18 to 16, thereby equalizing it with the age of consent for heterosexual activity.[2] In 1992, Israel's Equal Employment Opportunity Act was revised to prohibit discrimination in employment on the basis of sexual orientation and marital status.[3] In 1994, same-sex partners were afforded equal rights in the private sector and in 1997 were given equal rights in the public sector.[4] These rights include insurance, pension, and survivor benefits. In 2002, Tel Aviv passed a law making same-sex couples eligible for discounts and benefits at cultural facilities, libraries, swimming pools, and various city events.[5]

Although Israel does not give legal status to gay and lesbian couples, the government recognizes same-sex marriages performed in other countries and affords couples many legal benefits of marriage.[6] Same-sex couples have recently been permitted to adopt each other's children and are afforded privileges related to immigration.[7] A person in a same-sex relationship with a citizen can be granted a work permit which will be replaced by temporary resident status after one year.[8] After seven years, he or she can become a permanent resident. This time period is longer than that necessary for heterosexual married couples. While married couples receive their immigration rights through the Citizenship Law of 1952, unmarried couples receive their rights from the discretionary powers of the Ministry of Interior in the Law of Entry into Israel of 1952.[9]

Gays and lesbians have been allowed to serve in the Israeli military since Israel was founded in 1948.[10] In 1993, the military ended restrictions on the assignments gays and lesbians could be given.[11] A 2006 study found that 52 percent of gay and lesbian soldiers reported experiencing some form of sexual harassment during their service in the military.[12] The survey indicated that most of the harassment was verbal. A 2000 United States study found that the presence of gay and lesbian soldiers in the Israeli military does not affect combat readiness, unit cohesion, or military preparedness.[13]

Although the government has laws in place protecting the rights of gays and lesbians, homosexuality is not accepted within all religions and cultures.[14] There have been some reports of violence and discrimination directed at gays and lesbians, especially those suffering from HIV/AIDS. Gay Pride events and marches have been held often without disruption or violence, however there have been some instances of protests against these events.[15] In 2006, thousands of members of the Haredi community protested at Jerusalem's Sabbath Square over the holding of the city's Gay Pride Parade.[16] Many Palestinians have fled to Israel to escape persecution over their sexual orientation in spite of the threat of being detained and deported. There have been reports of the Israeli government coercing gay Palestinians to work undercover and subjecting them to torture and prostitution. They are often treated as security threats and treated with great caution.[17]

PUBLIC OPINION DATA[18]

In a 2007 poll, 38 percent of respondents believed that homosexuality should be accepted and 50 percent believed that it should be rejected.[19] A majority of Israeli respondents approve of granting pension and survivorship rights to same-sex partners, with 56 percent in 2007 stating that such a policy is either good or necessary.

Table 25.1: **What is your opinion on the following?**

		(In percent)			
Israel	Very Good	Somewhat Good	Not Good, but Necessary	Not Good	Total (N)
Granting pension and survivorship rights to same-sex partners					
2007	23	22	11	36	92 (609)

NOTES

1. U.S. Department of State, 2007 Country Reports on Human Rights Practices, Israel, March 11, 2008, available at: http://www.state.gov/g/drl/rls/hrrpt/2007/100597.htm (July 27, 2008); Baird, V. (2004). *Sex, Love & Homophobia*. United Kingdom: Amnesty International.

2. United States General Accounting Office, "Homosexuals in the Military: Policies and Practices of Foreign Countries," available at: http://dont.stanford.edu/regulations/GAO.pdf (July 20, 2008); IsRealli, available at: http://www.isrealli.org/gay-rights-in-israel/ (July 27, 2008).

3. IsRealli, available at: http://www.isrealli.org/gay-rights-in-israel/ (July 27, 2008).

4. Ibid.

5. International Gay and Lesbian Human Rights Commission, available at: http://www.iglhrc.org/site/iglhrc/content.php?type=1&id=91#AZCountry (July 22, 2008).

6. IsRealli, available at: http://www.isrealli.org/gay-rights-in-israel/ (July 27, 2008).

7. Ibid.

8. Human Rights Watch, available at: http://www.asylumlaw.org/docs/sexualminorities/HRWsamesexcouplesimmigration.pdf (July 27, 2008).

9. Ibid.

10. United States General Accounting Office, "Homosexuals in the Military: Policies and Practices of Foreign Countries," available at: http://dont.stanford.edu/regulations/GAO.pdf (July 20, 2008).

11. Ibid.

12. The Jerusalem Post, "Poll: 52% of gay soldiers sexually harassed in IDF," available at: http://www.jpost.com/servlet/Satellite?cid=1159193496955&pagename=JPost%2FJPArticle%2FShowFull (July 27, 2008).

13. Gay Law Net, available at: http://www.gaylawnet.com (July 27, 2008).

14. U.S. Department of State, 2007 Country Reports on Human Rights Practices, Israel, March 11, 2008, available at: http://www.state.gov/g/drl/rls/hrrpt/2007/100597.htm (July 27, 2008).

15. Ibid.

16. GLBTJews, "Haredim: J'lem gay parade may lead to another war," available at: http://www.glbtjews.org/article.php3?id_article=280 (July 27, 2008).

17. BBC News, "Palestinian gays flee to Israel," available at: http://news.bbc.co.uk/2/hi/middle_east/3211772.stm (July 27, 2008).

18. Data obtained from Angus Reid Global Monitor, available at: http://www.angus-reid.com/polls/view/israelis_ponder_rights_of_same_sex_unions/ (July 27, 2008)

19. Pew Global Attitudes Project, "World publics welcome global trade—but not Immigration," available at: http://pewglobal.org/reports/display.php?ReportID=258 (November 21, 2008).

26

Egypt

Egypt is a conservative, Islamic country that does not generally recognize the rights of its gay and lesbian citizens. Although Egyptian law does not explicitly refer to or criminalize homosexuality, authorities have often used laws related to obscenity and morality to arrest gays and lesbians.[1] Charges like debauchery and contempt of religion are often used to make arrests and carry maximum prison sentences of three and five years, respectively.[2] Because Islam heavily influences the Egyptian government, the law often makes references to religion and classifies as crimes actions that go against religious principles, including homosexuality. Since gays and lesbians are often not tolerated by the government, same-sex couples do not enjoy legal recognition or benefits. In addition, single women and lesbian partners are not allowed to receive treatment for artificial insemination.[3] Egypt's refusal to recognize same-sex partners also leaves these couples with no privileges in regard to immigration. Additionally, Egypt does not recognize persecution due to one's sexual orientation as a basis for asylum applications.[4] Although Egypt is often believed to be intolerant of its gay and lesbian population, the government has taken steps to address public health issues. In an effort to combat the country's growing HIV/AIDS population, the government runs a confidential HIV hotline that provides callers with information about HIV/AIDS.[5]

Over the past few years, there have been many publicized arrests of people as a function of their sexual orientation. In 2000, two men were arrested for drawing up a legally unrecognized marriage contract.[6] One of the men was held on charges of practicing immoral and indecent behavior and was later released. The other man was charged with "violation of honor by threat." An incident in 2001 involving the arrest of fifty-two men, informally named the Cairo 52, drew international attention to the treatment of gays and lesbians in Egypt.[7] All of the men were arrested while onboard a floating nightclub called the Queen Boat and were brought to trial on charges of habitual practice of debauchery and contempt of religion.[8] International human rights organizations and country leaders expressed concern over the men's treatment while in custody and discrimination exhibited by the Egyptian government. After the men's trials, twenty-three of the fifty-two were convicted and sentenced to between one and five years of hard labor.[9] In 2003, an Israeli tourist was arrested in Cairo, interrogated, and held in prison for several days allegedly due to his perceived status as a gay man.[10]

The intolerance of gays and lesbians has influenced Egypt's human rights organizations which defend the rights of women, minority Christians, and prisoners. Leaders of these organizations explain that Egyptians do not stand for gay rights, making it difficult for them to follow through with their missions.[11] International human rights groups have accused the Egyptian government of trying to silence local groups by limiting their main source of revenue, foreign funding, and arresting activists.[12] In a 2007 poll, only 1 percent of respondents believed that homosexuality should be accepted and 95 percent believed that it should be rejected.[13]

NOTES

1. U.S. Department of State, 2007 Country Reports on Human Rights Practices, Egypt, March 11, 2008, available at: http://www.state.gov/g/drl/rls/hrrpt/2007/100594.htm (July 22, 2008); GayMiddleEast.com, available at: http://www.gaymiddleeast.com/country/egypt (July 22, 2008).

2. GayMiddleEast.com, available at: http://www.gaymiddleeast.com/country/egypt (July 22, 2008).

3. ILGA, World Legal Wrap-Up Survey, available at: http://www.ilga.org/statehomophobia/World_legal_wrap_up_survey_November2006.pdf (July 22, 2008).

4. Ibid.

5. POZ, "Egypt Combats Stigma Through HIV Hotline," available at: http://www.poz.com/articles/egypt_hiv_stigma_1_13656.shtml (July 22, 2008).

6. Sodomy Laws, available at: http://www.sodomylaws.org/world/egypt/egnews01.htm (July 22, 2008).

7. Homosexuality in Egypt, available at: http://www.mtholyoke.edu/~appel20l/classweb/Cairo%2052.html (July 22, 2008); International Gay and Lesbian Human Rights Commission, available at: http://www.iglhrc.org/site/iglhrc/section.php?id=5&detail=82 (July 22, 2008).

8. Ibid.

9. Ibid.

10. GayMiddleEast.com, available at: http://www.gaymiddleeast.com/news/article19.htm (July 22, 2008).

11. "Egyptian rights group 'cannot protect gays'," BBC News, available at: http://news.bbc.co.uk/2/hi/middle_east/1813926.stm (November 3, 2008).

12. Ibid.

13. Pew Global Attitudes Project, "World publics welcome global trade—but not Immigration," available at: http://pewglobal.org/reports/display.php?ReportID=258 (November 21, 2008).</notes>

㉗

Iran

Iran is a conservative Islamic country that, under Shari'a law, prohibits homosexuality and prescribes execution as a sanction.[1] In fact, Islamic law states that all sexual acts outside of a heterosexual marriage are forbidden.[2] The punishment for a non-Muslim homosexual is harsher than if he or she is a Muslim.[3] There have been many cases in which gays and lesbians have been punished or executed over their sexual orientation that have drawn the attention of the international community. In 2005, two teenagers aged 15 and 17 were witnessed engaging in homosexual acts and were hanged for perverting Islamic law.[4] In 2004, Iran's judiciary formed the Special Protection Division, intended to monitor and report moral crimes.[5]

In 2007, during a speech at Columbia University, President Mahmoud Ahmadinejad denied the presence of homosexuals in Iran.[6] His comments drew criticism from many gay and lesbian advocacy groups and international organizations. Presidential aides later said that he was misquoted and meant that Iran has a lower number of gays and lesbians than the United States.[7] Although Iran discriminates against its gay and lesbian population, the country has allowed sex change operations since the Ayatollah Ruhollah Khomeini passed a fatwa authorizing them approximately twenty-five years ago.[8] Although military service is mandatory for men in Iran, gay men are allowed medical dispensations from mandatory military service.[9]

Gays and lesbians in Iran have faced difficulty finding asylum in other countries. In March of 2008, the Netherlands rejected an Iranian's request for asylum submitted on the basis that he faced persecution in Iran over his sexual orientation.[10] His petition for asylum had previously been rejected in Great Britain and due to an

EU regulation, his application generally cannot be considered in any other EU countries.

PUBLIC OPINION DATA

There is no public opinion data to report for Iran.

NOTES

1. Gay Law Net, available at: http://www.gaylawnet.com (July 29, 2008).

2. Pink News, "Moscow bans demonstration outside Iranian embassy," available at: http://www.pinknews.co.uk/news/articles/2005-8348.html (July 28, 2008).

3. U.S. Department of State, 2007 Country Reports on Human Rights Practices, Iran, March 11, 2008, available at: http://www.state.gov/g/drl/rls/hrrpt/2007/100595.htm (July 28, 2008).

4. Pink News, "Moscow bans demonstration outside Iranian embassy," available at: http://www.pinknews.co.uk/news/articles/2005-8348.html (July 28, 2008).

5. U.S. Department of State, 2007 Country Reports on Human Rights Practices, Iran, March 11, 2008, available at: http://www.state.gov/g/drl/rls/hrrpt/2007/100595.htm (July 28, 2008).

6. Reuters, "President misquoted over gays in Iran," available at: http://www.reuters.com/article/worldNews/idUSBLA05294620071010 (July 28, 2008).

7. Ibid.

8. *The Guardian*, "Sex change funding undermines no gays claim," available at: http://www.guardian.co.uk/world/2007/sep/26/iran.gender (July 28, 2008).

9. Fox News, "Iran does far worse than ignore gays, critics say," available at: http://www.foxnews.com/story/0,2933,297982,00.html (July 28, 2008).

10. CNN, "Gay Iranian teen loses asylum appeal," available at: http://edition.cnn.com/2008/WORLD/meast/03/11/iran.asylum/ (July 29, 2008).

(28)

Nigeria

Homosexuality is illegal in Nigeria, a country whose dominating religions include Christianity and Islam.[1] Homosexual acts are punished by up to fourteen years in prison and, in the northern states under Shari'a law, are punishable by execution by stoning.[2] Although laws expressly prohibit consensual sex between men, the law does not mention sex between women.[3] There is widespread violence and discrimination directed toward the country's gay and lesbian population. Discrimination is especially pervasive for the many people living with HIV/AIDS; people have been fired from their jobs and denied medical treatment due to their disease that is viewed by many as having stemmed from immoral behavior.[4] Nigeria's government recently considered a law that would have explicitly prohibited same-sex marriage, imposing a sentence of five years in prison for anyone involved in the performance of such a ceremony.[5] The bill would have also prohibited the adoption of children by same-sex couples and imposed prison terms for public advocacy of gay and lesbian rights.[6] Many human rights organizations condemned the bill which eventually was not passed.[7]

Reported arrests of gays and lesbians are fairly common. Over a dozen citizens have been sentenced to death for prohibited sex acts including homosexuality since Shari'a law was enacted in 2000 in northern Nigeria.[8] The Shari'a court recently sentenced several women to prison terms and 20 lashes for involvement in lesbian relationships, claiming they violated the tenets of Islam and Shari'a law.[9] Since homosexuality is illegal and same-sex relationships are not legally recognized, gays and lesbians do not enjoy privileges related to immigration, asylum, or adoption.[10] In a 2007 poll, only 2 percent of respondents believed that homosexuality should be accepted and 97 percent believed that it should be rejected.[11]

NOTES

1. U.S. Department of State, 2007 Country Reports on Human Rights Practices, Nigeria, March 11, 2008, available at: http://www.state.gov/g/drl/rls/hrrpt/2007/100498.htm (July 27, 2008).

2. Ibid.

3. Gay Law Net, available at: http://www.gaylawnet.com (July 27, 2008).

4. Ibid.

5. Ibid.

6. Ibid.

7. PinkNews, "March date for Sharia 'gay' trial in Nigeria," available at: http://www.pinknews.co.uk/news/articles/2005-6878.html (July 27, 2008).

8. Gay Law Net, available at: http://www.gaylawnet.com (July 27, 2008).

9. Ibid.

10. Partners Task Force, available at: http://buddybuddy.com/immigr.html (July 27, 2008).

11. Pew Global Attitudes Project, "World publics welcome global trade—but not Immigration," available at: http://pewglobal.org/reports/display.php?ReportID=258 (November 21, 2008).

South Africa

The history of South Africa's treatment of gays and lesbians has evolved over time due to the end of apartheid. The apartheid government criminalized homosexuality and punished it with sentences of up to seven years in prison.[1] The government was wary of homosexual behavior and subjected men to aversion therapy to deter homosexuality.[2] The postapartheid government later passed the country's constitution which became the first in the world to prohibit discrimination on the basis of sexual orientation.[3] The country also made the age of consent for sexual activity equal at 16 for both heterosexual and homosexual relations.[4] In 2006, South Africa made history again by becoming the first country in Africa and fifth in the world to legalize same-sex marriage.[5] The countries that previously had legalized same-sex marriage were Netherlands, Belgium, Spain, and Canada.[6] The law allows religious institutions and civil officers to refuse to conduct same-sex marriage ceremonies if it contradicts their beliefs and customs.[7]

In 1999, South Africa's Constitutional Court overturned legislation restricting immigration benefits to opposite-sex spouses while denying the benefits to same-sex partners.[8] As a result, the country's immigration laws were amended and same-sex couples are now afforded the same rights as heterosexual, married couples. In 2002, South Africa's Constitutional Court ruled that gay and lesbian couples are entitled to adopt children.[9] There are no written laws or policies regarding the service of gays and lesbians in the military.[10] There have been no recent official reports of violence or discrimination against gays and lesbians.[11] Currently, gays and lesbians enjoy the same freedoms as other citizens and deal with a low level of violence and discrimination in comparison to many other countries. In a 2007 poll, 28 percent of respondents believed that homosexuality should be accepted and 64 percent believed that it should be rejected.[12]

NOTES

1. BBC News, "Gay Rights Win in South Africa," available at: http://news.bbc.co.uk/2/hi/africa/190268.stm (July 20, 2008).

2. Ibid.

3. Constitutional Court of South Africa, available at: http://www.concourt.gov.za/text/rights/know/homosexual.html (July 20, 2008).

4. Avert.org, available at: http://www.avert.org/aofconsent.htm (July 20, 2008).

5. Equal Marriage for Same-Sex Couples, available at: http://www.samesexmarriage.ca/equality/saf301106.htm (July 20, 2008).

6. Catholic News Agency, available at: http://www.catholicnewsagency.com/new.php?n=4433 (July 7, 2008).

7. Pew Forum, Same-Sex Marriage: Redefining Marriage Around the World, available at: http://pewforum.org/docs/?DocID=235 (July 20, 2008).

8. Human Rights Watch, Resource Library, available at: http://hrw.org/english/docs/2007/07/11/global16374.htm (July 20, 2008).

9. Windy City Media Group, "South Africa OKs adoption," available at: http://www.windycitymediagroup.com/gay/lesbian/news/ARTICLE.php?AID=1187 (July 20, 2008).

10. United States General Accounting Office, "Homosexuals in the Military: Policies and Practices of Foreign Countries," available at: http://dont.stanford.edu/regulations/GAO.pdf (July 20, 2008).

11. U.S. Department of State, 2007 Country Reports on Human Rights Practices, South Africa, March 11, 2008, available at: http://www.state.gov/g/drl/rls/hrrpt/2007/100505.htm (July 20, 2008).

12. Pew Global Attitudes Project, "World publics welcome global trade—but not Immigration," available at: http://pewglobal.org/reports/display.php?ReportID=258 (November 21, 2008).

ⒿⓄ

India

India punishes homosexuality in Section 377 of its Penal Code, banning it and other "unnatural offenses" including bestiality.[1] Homosexual activity is punishable with up to life imprisonment. This conduct is illegal in spite of India's ratification of the International Covenant on Civil and Political Rights (ICCPR) whose provisions protect same-sex sexual relations between consenting adults.[2] As a result of homosexuality being illegal, same-sex couples receive no legal recognition. Gays and lesbians are also not allowed to adopt children.[3]

India frequently deals with hostility directed towards its gay and lesbian community. Human Rights Watch reports instances where the police have used Section 377 of the India Penal Code to harass gay men and hinder HIV/AIDS prevention efforts.[4] Gays and lesbians have faced discrimination in several areas of society, particularly through employment discrimination.[5] Activists report that homosexuals who do not conceal their sexual orientation are often fired from their jobs.[6] In addition to violent acts perpetrated by Indian citizens, the police have reportedly committed crimes against gays and lesbians. The HIV/AIDS population has reported experiencing discrimination through expulsion from school and denial of housing due to their HIV status. Estimates on the number of people infected by HIV/AIDS is approximately 5.1 million.[7] A campaign called Voices Against 377 is working to overturn Section 377 which bans homosexuality.[8]

Recently, human rights organizations are attempting to overrule Section 377 due to the prevalence of gays being blackmailed in India.[9] These groups have brought their challenge of the law to the New Delhi High Court and the verdict is expected before the end of 2008. Because homosexuality is illegal in India, many people are taking advantage of others by posing as gays in Internet chat rooms, subsequently black-mailing people they meet for money in exchange for not turning them in to the police. Many people give in to their demands due to both the possibility of arrest and the social stigma of being gay that is pervasive in Indian society. In fact, it is common for gay men to marry in spite of their sexual orientation, due to the intense pressure to get married and to avoid the consequences of being publicly gay. Human rights groups argue that this harassment of gays and lesbians will continue until the law is amended to decriminalize homosexuality. In a 2007 poll, 81 percent of respondents believed that homosexuality should be rejected and 10 percent believed it should be accepted.[10]

NOTES

1. Gay Law Net, available at: http://www.gaylawnet.com/ (June 22, 2008).

2. Ibid.

3. Children's Home Society & Family Services, India Adoption Require-ments, available at: http://www.childrenshomeadopt.org/India_Adoption_Requirements.html (June 23, 2008).

4. Human Rights Watch, India: Repeal Colonial-Era Sodomy Law, avail-able at: http://hrw.org/english/docs/2006/01/11/india12398.htm

5. U.S. Department of State, 2007 Country Reports on Human Rights Practices, India, March 11, 2008, available at: http://www.state.gov/g/drl/rls/hrrpt/2007/100614.htm (June 22, 2008).

6. Ibid.

7. Ibid.

8. Ibid.

9. See "For Gays in India, Fear Rules," The Washington Post, available at: http://www.washingtonpost.com/wp-dyn/content/article/2008/11/14/AR2008111403645_pf.html (November 17, 2008).

10. Pew Global Attitudes Project, "World publics welcome global trade—but not Immigration," available at: http://pewglobal.org/reports/display.php?ReportID=258 (November 21, 2008).

31

China

The Chinese government's treatment of gays has steadily improved since China's Cultural Revolution.[1] According to the Ministry of Health, China has approximately 30 million homosexuals between the ages of fifteen and sixty.[2] Homosexuality was decriminalized in 1997 and was removed from the list of mental illnesses in 2001.[3] In the Penal Code of 1979, homosexual acts were considered to be "hooliganism." In 1993 the Ministry of Public Security directed that homosexuals would no longer be charged under the hooliganism paragraph which was later repealed in 1997.[4] Hong Kong decriminalized homosexual acts in 1991.[5] Shanghai's Fudan University introduced its first undergraduate course on homosexuality in 2005.[6]

Although there are no laws criminalizing private homosexual activity between consenting adults, there is pressure to conform to family and cultural expectations that discourage homosexuality.[7] Several reports have found that more than 80 percent of gay men married because of social pressure.[8] In response to high rates of HIV infections, the government launched support and awareness campaigns, including one to provide emotional, psychological, and legal help to citizens.[9] However, the media are heavily censored by the government and this may contribute to the low number of people who take advantage of the national services.[10]

China does not recognize same-sex marriage but considered legislation in 2003 that would have made unions legal.[11] Because China does not give legal status to same-sex partners, couples are not given privileges in regards to immigration or asylum.[12] China's adoption law specifically identifies partners that adopt children as being husband and wife.[13] Furthermore, gays and lesbians are banned from donating blood due to their high-risk status for contracting HIV.[14]

Table 31.1: Do you agree or disagree with the following?

China		Agree	Partially Agree/Disagree	Disagree	Total (N)
			(In percent)		
There is something wrong with homosexuality					
	2008	40	30	20	90 (400)
I would be friends with a homosexual					
	2008	60	-	30	90 (400)
Same-sex marriage					
	2008	30	-	70	100 (400)
Gay-themed movies or TV shows ought to be openly shown in China					
	2008	55	-	40	95 (400)
Equal employment rights for gays and lesbians					
	2008	91	-	-	91 (400)

PUBLIC OPINION DATA[15]

In a 2007 poll, 17 percent of respondents believed that homosexuality should be accepted and 69 percent believed that it should be rejected.[16] A plurality of Chinese respondents believed there is something wrong with homosexuality (40 percent in 2008). In addition, a majority would be friends with a homosexual (60 percent in 2008) and believed that gays and lesbians should enjoy equal employment rights (91 percent in 2008). Furthermore, a majority believed that gay-themed movies or TV shows ought to be openly shown in China (55 percent in 2008) but a minority believed that same-sex marriage should be legal (30 percent in 2008).

NOTES

1. Gay Life in China, available at: http://gaylife.about.com/od/world/a/chinachinesein.htm (July 3, 2008).

2. U.S. Department of State, 2006 Country Reports on Human Rights Practices, China, March 6, 2007, available at: http://www.state.gov/g/drl/rls/hrrpt/2007/100518.htm (July 3, 2008).

3. Gay Law Net, available at: http://www.gaylawnet.com/ (July 3, 2008).

4. International Lesbian and Gay Association, available at: http://www
.ilga.org/statehomophobia/World_legal_wrap_up_survey_November2006.pdf
(July 3, 2008).

5. Ibid.

6. Gay Life in China, available at: http://gaylife.about.com/od/world/a/
chinachinesein.htm (July 3, 2008).

7. U.S. Department of State, 2007 Country Reports on Human Rights
Practices, China, March 11, 2008, available at: http://www.state.gov/g/drl/rls/
hrrpt/2007/100518.htm (July 3, 2008).

8. Ibid.

9. Gay Life in China, available at: http://gaylife.about.com/od/world/a/
chinachinesein.htm (July 3, 2008).

10. Ibid.

11. Same Sex Marriage: A Global Review, available at: http://i2r.org/fmm/
issues/september2005/article2.html (July 3, 2008).

12. Immigration Roundup, available at: http://www.buddybuddy.com/
immigr.html (July 3, 2008).

13. Adoption Law of the People's Republic of China, available at:
http://www.china-ccaa.org/site percent5Cinfocontent percent5CZCFG_
2005100901425793_en.htm (July 3, 2008).

14. Chinese Homosexuals Banned from Donating Blood, available at:
http://us.oneworld.net/places/palau/-/article/chinese-homosexuals-banned
-donating-blood (July 3, 2008).

15. Data obtained from "Li Yinhe on Chinese attitudes towards homosexuality," available at: http://peijinchen.com/blog/2008/06/18/li-yinhe-on
-chinese-attitudes-towards-homosexuality-ten-questions/ (July 3, 2008).

16. Pew Global Attitudes Project, "World publics welcome global trade—
but not Immigration," available at: http://pewglobal.org/reports/display
.php?ReportID=258 (November 21, 2008).

㉜

Japan

Japanese society has largely succeeded in repressing the country's small movement advocating equal rights for gay and lesbian citizens. Same-sex partnerships receive no legal recognition and, in general, gays and lesbians have not brought challenges to the Japanese court system over the lack of such recognition.[1] Consensual sex between same-sex couples has been legal in Japan since 1882.[2] Although homosexuality is legal, Japanese society is not welcoming to people who publicize their homosexual status, making it difficult for people to advocate for gay and lesbian rights.[3] Without legal recognition, gay and lesbian partners have the option to adopt their partners or draw up contracts giving their partners rights to their finances, property, and children.[4] Japan does not provide special accommodations to gays and lesbians in regard to immigration or asylum.[5] The Tokyo District Court held in 2004 that an Iranian man's sexual orientation was not sufficient grounds to grant him refugee status.[6]

Parts of the Japanese government have recently begun to ban discrimination on the basis of sexual orientation. In 2001, the Council for Human Rights Promotion of the Japanese Justice Ministry explicitly included discrimination based on sexual orientation within the mandate of the proposed national human rights commission.[7] In 2000, the Tokyo Metropolitan Government included sexual orientation as a category protected from discrimination within its new human rights guidelines.[8] Additionally, the governments of Tokyo and Ehime mention gay and lesbian rights in their cities' human rights guidelines.[9] In a 2007 poll, 49 percent of respondents believed that homosexuality should be accepted and 28 percent believed that it should be rejected.[10]

Japan has no written regulations or policies in place addressing gays and lesbians serving in the military, the Japanese Defense Force.[11] However, this does not mean that the government openly accepts gays and lesbians into the military. Japanese government officials have indicated that known homosexuals may not be selected to enter the military and people found engaging in homosexual activities while in the military could be reassigned.[12]

NOTES

1. Andenæs, M. T., Wintemute, R., & Andenas, M. (2001). *Legal recognition of same-sex partnerships*. Oxford: Hart Publishing.

2. Gay Law Net, available at: http://www.gaylawnet.com/ (August 22, 2008).

3. Baird, V. (2004). *Sex, love & homophobia*. Amnesty International UK; Andenæs, M. T., Wintemute, R., & Andenas, M. (2001). *Legal recognition of same-sex partnerships*. Oxford: Hart Publishing.

4. Andenæs, M. T., Wintemute, R., & Andenas, M. (2001). *Legal recognition of same-sex partnerships*. Oxford: Hart Publishing.

5. Partners Task Force, "Immigration Roundup," available at: http://buddybuddy.com/immigr.html (August 22, 2008).

6. Gay Law Net, available at: http://www.gaylawnet.com/ (August 21, 2008).

7. Ibid.

8. Ibid.

9. Ibid.

10. Pew Global Attitudes Project, "World publics welcome global trade—but not Immigration," available at: http://pewglobal.org/reports/display.php?ReportID=258 (November 21, 2008).

11. United States General Accounting Office, "Homosexuals in the Military: Policies and Practices of Foreign Countries," available at: http://dont.stanford.edu/regulations/GAO.pdf (July 20, 2008).

12. Ibid.

㉝ Australia

Australia's laws regarding gays and lesbian rights vary amongst its states. In regard to same-sex marriage, although there are no federal provisions for registered partnership or civil union laws, some states extend many rights to gay and lesbian couples. In 2004 the Australian government passed the Marriage Amendment Act which declared that same-sex marriages would not be recognized in the country.[1] The Act also specifically mentioned that the legislation should not provide for the adoption of children by same-sex couples.[2]

Through the Civil Partnerships Act of 2008, the Australian Capital Territory (ACT) provides legal recognition of couples, regardless of sex, through registered partnerships.[3] A couple may be recognized in this manner if the relationship is not prohibited (i.e., the couple are not lineal ancestors of each other, siblings, or half-siblings) and both people live within the ACT.[4] In 2004, the ACT began to allow same-sex couples to adopt children.[5] In New South Wales, legislation passed in 2008 will recognize co-mothers as legal parents of children born through the use of artificial insemination, birth certificates will be issued recognizing both mothers, and same-sex couples will be protected from discrimination in employment and access to goods and services.[6] In Queensland, same-sex couples can be recognized as "de facto" partners for legal purposes.[7] South Australia's Domestic Partners Act of 2006 gave same-sex couples financial, inheritance, and next of kin rights.[8] In 2004, Tasmania became the first state to create a domestic partnership registry for same-sex couples to be recognized legally.[9] Tasmania's Relationship Act of 2003 extended many rights given to opposite-sex couples such as rights to hospital visitation, wills, and parenting and bereavement leave.[10] The states of Victoria and Western Australia recognize same-sex couples as de-facto couples and allow them to register their relationships.[11] In Western Australia, same-sex couples are allowed to adopt and receive access to infertility treatment.[12] In addition, lesbian partners who have a child through artificial insemination can both be listed on the birth certificate.[13]

Australia affords gays and lesbians many rights in terms of immigration and refugee application. Australia accepts applications from gays and lesbians for refugee status based on persecution and has recognized more than a hundred gays and lesbians as refugees.[14] Australia also gives same-sex couples special rights in regards to immigration. If a person has been in a "long term interdependent relationship" with a citizen for over five years, the typical two year waiting period from the time he or she is issued a temporary visa to the time permanent resident status is granted is waived.[15] In order to be considered in an interdependent relationship, the two people must not be related to each other, be over 18 years of age, have an exclusive and committed relationship with the other, and must live together.[16] The couple must still be in the relationship at the time citizenship is granted and must have been together for at least 12 months at the time of application.[17]

Australia has allowed gays and lesbians to serve in the military (Australian Defence Force) since 1992 and, in 2005, extended equal partner and family benefits to personnel in same-sex relationships.[18] In September 2000, the Center for the Study of Sexual Minorities in the Military (CSSMM) issued a report concluding that the lifting of the ban on gays and lesbians in the military has not led to any identifiable negative effects on troop morale, combat effectiveness, recruitment and retention, or other measures of military performance.[19] But a 1998 court ruling gave the ADF the authority to discriminate against HIV-positive military personnel because of the risk they posed in regard to spreading the virus.[20]

There have not been many reports of discrimination of citizens based on sexual orientation. The Australian Human Rights and Equal Opportunity Commission reported in 2007 that there are many federal laws that deny same-sex couples and their children benefits afforded to heterosexual couples and their children. The 1992 Disability Discrimination Act makes it illegal to discriminate against a person on the basis of the person's HIV or AIDS status and the Workplace Relations Act of 1996 makes it illegal to dismiss a person on the basis of his or her sexual orientation.[21] Also in 2007, there were nine reported assaults on gays and lesbians in Sydney.[22]

Table 33.1:   Do you agree or disagree with the following?

Australia	(In percent)		
	Agree	*Disagree*	*Total (N)*
Same-sex couples should have the same legal rights as heterosexual partners in common-law marriages			
2007	71	23	94
			(1000)
Same-sex couples should be allowed to get married			
2007	57	37	94
			(1000)

PUBLIC OPINION DATA[23]

A majority of Australian respondents believe that same-sex couples should have the same legal rights as heterosexual partners in common-law marriages (71 percent in 2007). A smaller majority favor allowing same-sex couples to get married (57 percent in 2007).

NOTES

1. Commonwealth of Australia Bills, available at: http://www.austlii.edu.au/au/legis/cth/bill/mlab2004287/ (July 17, 2008).

2. Ibid.

3. Gay Law Net, available at: http://www.gaylawnet.com/ (July 17, 2008).

4. *Australian Capital Territory Consolidated Acts*, available at: http://www.austlii.edu.au/au/legis/act/consol_act/cpa2008222/ (July 17, 2008).

5. Planetout.com, available at: http://www.planetout.com/news/article.html?2007/08/02/2 (July 17, 2008).

6. Inside Out Australia, available at: http://www.samesame.com.au/news/local/2328/New-Laws-For-Same-Sex-Families.htm (July 17, 2008).

7. Discrimination Law Amendment Act 2002, available at: http://www.legislation.qld.gov.au/LEGISLTN/ACTS/2002/02AC074.pdf (July 17, 2008).

8. Gaywired.com, available at: http://www.gaywired.com/article.cfm?section=66&id=11930 (July 17, 2008).

9. 365gay.com, available at: http://www.365gay.com/Newscon08/06/062008oz.htm (July 17, 2008).

10. Partners Task Force, available at: http://www.buddybuddy.com/d-p-taz.html (July 17, 2008).

11. TypePad, available at: http://samesexmarriage.typepad.com/weblog/2008/04/australia-victo.html (July 17, 2008).

12. http://www.letsgetequal.org.au/Info-legislative-recognition-same-sex-relationshipsAU.doc (July 17, 2008).

13. Ibid.

14. Glbtq, available at: http://www.glbtq.com/social-sciences/immigration_law.html; Gay Law Net, available at: http://www.gaylawnet.com/ (July 17, 2008).

15. Gay and Lesbian Immigration Taskforce, available at: http://www.glitf.org.au/index.php?option=com_content&task=view&id=23&Itemid=32 (July 17, 2008).

16. Ibid.

17. Ibid.

18. Australian Coalition for Equality, available at: http://www.coalitionforequality.org.au/index.php?option=com_content&task=view&id=162&Itemid=1 (July 17, 2008).

19. Gay Law Net, available at: http://www.gaylawnet.com/ (July 17, 2008).

20. Ibid.

21. Gay Law Net, available at: http://www.gaylawnet.com/ (July 17, 2008).

22. U.S. Department of State, 2007 Country Reports on Human Rights Practices, Australia, March 11, 2008, available at: http://www.state.gov/g/drl/rls/hrrpt/2007/100513.htm (July 17, 2008).

23. Data obtained from Angus Reid Global Monitor, available at: http://www.angus-reid.com/polls/view/australians_back_same_sex_marriage/ (June 29, 2008). (June 2, 2008).

Gay and Lesbian Adoption

While many gay and lesbian adults and couples are interested in adopting children, discrimination throughout the adoption process has made it difficult for gays and lesbians to successfully adopt.[1] However, research supports the belief that gay and lesbian parents are not poor parents in comparison to heterosexual adults and couples. Findings by a nonpartisan adoption group conclude that gays and lesbians are an important resource for children awaiting adoption. There is near "universal professional consensus" that these applicants should be judged on their qualifications, not sexual orientation.[2] Lesbian mothers have been found to be comparable to heterosexual mothers in their desire to be good parents, and provide warmth toward their children.[3]

Gay fathers have been found to be comparable to heterosexual fathers in involvement and intimacy with their children, encouragement of autonomy, problem-solving and parental satisfaction, and superior to other fathers in the way they respond to their child's needs and in their communication of reasons for appropriate behavior.[4] In comparison to children raised by heterosexual parents, children raised by gay and lesbian parents have been found to be similar in intelligence, moral development, and involvement in peer relationships.[5] Additionally, children have no apparent adjustment problems related to their parent's sexual orientation.

Around the world, countries vary in the level of rights they provide to gay and lesbian couples in terms of adoption. Countries that allow adoption include Germany, Spain, Great Britain, South Africa, Israel, and Sweden. Countries that do not allow gays and lesbians to adopt include Italy, Argentina, Brazil, Hungary, Russia, Poland, India, and Iran. Other countries' laws are either vague, do not explicitly address same-sex parent adoption, or vary according to jurisdiction.

In France, the European Court of Human Rights overturned French court rulings that prevented a single lesbian woman from adopting a child.[6] Gay and lesbian advocacy groups believe this opens the way for legal challenges in other European states with adoption laws similar to those in France, yet it falls short of a blanket ruling that would force all countries to allow adoption by homosexuals. The court faulted the French courts for citing "the lack of a paternal referent in the household," and said the woman's homosexuality had been "if not explicit, at least implicit" in France's rejection of her adoption request.[7] The court found that France had violated the European Convention on Human Rights—to which France and the other forty-six Council of Europe members are signatories—by failing to assess adoption by a lesbian the same way it would a single heterosexual. The judgment forced France to allow the plaintiff, a forty-five-year-old nursery school teacher who has lived with her female partner for nearly twenty years, to adopt, and ordered France to pay $14,600 in damages and $21,210 in legal costs.[8] In a previous 2002 case, Fretté v. France, the European Court of Human Rights had ruled, four votes to three, that preventing a gay man from applying to adopt a child because of his sexual orientation did not violate the convention.[9]

In Argentina, civil unions are granted in the city of Buenos Aires and the province of Río Negro and give legal rights similar to those for heterosexual couples, excluding adoption and inheritance rights.[10] In 2008, Brazil's lower house of Congress rejected part of an adoption bill that would have allowed same-sex couples to adopt children.[11] A proposal that would grant same-sex couples the same rights as married heterosexuals has been stalled for more than ten years in Brazil's Congress. The adoption bill will return to Brazil's Senate for further debate. In Canada, provinces and territories govern adoption and so the law is not uniform throughout the country. Adoption by same-sex couples is legal in British Columbia, Manitoba, Newfoundland and Labrador, Nova Scotia, Ontario, Quebec, Saskatchewan, the Northwest Territories, New Brunswick, Prince Edward Island, and Nunavut. In Alberta, stepchild adoption is allowed.[12] In Hungary, same-sex couples can receive many rights of marriage through common-law marriages. However, Hungary's cohabitation law does not provide same-sex couples access to adoption.[13] In Spain, same-sex couples are permitted to marry and adopt children.[14]

In Sweden, gay couples registered in a legal partnership—permitted in Sweden since 1995—are able to adopt children both within the country and from abroad.[15] Previously, a single parent could adopt a child after passing a battery of tests and if there was another person of the opposite sex willing to commit to providing a gender role model for the child.[16] In Great Britain, any unmarried couple, including a same-sex couple, wishing to adopt must demonstrate that their partnership is an "enduring family relationship."[17] Same-sex marriage is illegal in Russia. Marriage traditions are heavily influenced by the Russian Orthodox Church that sees homosexuality as a perversion and has prohibited adoption by gay and lesbian couples.[18]

Adoption laws in Australia vary by states and territories. In Western Australia, same-sex couples are allowed to adopt and receive access to infertility treatment.[19] In 2004, the Australian Capital Terriroty began to allow same-sex couples to adopt children.[20] In Tasmania, only stepparent adoption is allowed.[21] In New South Wales, same-sex couples cannot jointly adopt but single gay or lesbian individuals are permitted.[22] In Queensland, same-sex couples cannot legally adopt a child, but can become foster parents.[23]

In 2002, South Africa's Constitutional Court ruled that gay and lesbian couples are entitled to adopt children.[24] In Israel, the law grants members of same sex unions the right to adopt their partner's children and be considered their legal guardians.[25] The Same Sex Marriage (Prohibition) Act was introduced in the Nigerian Assembly in 2006. The bill would provide for a five year prison term to anyone who "goes through the ceremony of marriage with a person of the same sex," "performs, witnesses, aids or abets the ceremony of same sex marriage" or "is involved in the registration of gay clubs, societies and organizations, sustenance, procession or meetings, publicity and public show of same sex amorous relationship directly or indirectly in public and in private." The law would also prohibit adoption of children by lesbian or gay couples or individuals.[26] The Nigerian Assembly failed to bring the bill to a final vote and the bill died at the end of the legislative session, pending potential reintroduction.[27] China's adoption law specifically identifies partners that adopt children as being husband and wife.[28] In Italy, India, and Poland, gays and lesbians are not permitted to adopt children.[29]

In the United States, each state has its own "adoption statute," enacted by the state legislature, which provides the general procedures and policies for adoptions in that state.[30] While states may restrict adoption by sexual orientation or marital status, a federal judge has ruled that states must recognize out-of-state adoptions even if they would be illegal if performed in their state, due to the Full Faith and Credit Clause.[31]

Two states (Mississippi and Utah) have passed statutes that effectively bar same-sex couples from adopting but do not expressly bar single parent gay or lesbian adoption. Until recently, Florida was the only state that expressly barred adoptions by gay and lesbians—both as individuals and couples. In 2008, a Florida court overturned the law, stating that the best interests of children are not preserved by prohibiting adoption by gays and lesbians.[32] In the 2008 general election, Arkansas voters approved a ballot measure to create a law providing that an individual "cohabiting with a sexual partner outside of a [valid] marriage" may not adopt or serve as a foster parent.[33] More than a dozen families have filed a lawsuit challenging the law.[34]

In nearly all states and the District of Columbia, adoption statutes provide for "stepparent" adoptions. A stepparent adoption occurs when one individual petitions to adopt the child of his or her spouse without divesting the spouse of his or her own parental rights. Stepparent adoptions are a statutory exception to the general rule that when a child is adopted, the child's legal relationship with his or her preadoption parent(s) is terminated. For gays and lesbians, stepparent adoptions are generally unavailable because the adoption statutes of most states permit such adoptions only in the case of a legally married couple.

NOTES

1. Adoption by Gay and Lesbian Adults and Couples, available at: http://www.socialworkblog.org/helpstartshere/index.php/2008/page/2/ (January 13, 2008).

2. Chicago Tribune, "Study supports gay adoptions," available at: http://archives.chicagotribune.com/2008/sep/25/local/chi-gay-adoption-25-sep25 (January 16, 2009).

3. Adoption by Gay and Lesbian Adults and Couples, available at: http://www.socialworkblog.org/helpstartshere/index.php/2008/page/2/ (January 13, 2008).

4. Ibid.

5. Ibid.

6. Crumley-Paris, B. "France Overruled on Gay Adoption," available at: http://www.time.com/time/world/article/0,8599,1706514,00.html (January 14, 2008).

7. Ibid.

8. Ibid.

9. Human Rights Watch, Europe: Gay Adoption Ruling Advances Family Equality," available at: http://www.hrw.org/en/news/2008/01/23/europe-gay-adoption-ruling-advances-family-equality (January 15, 2008).

10. BBC News, "Gay marriage around the globe," available at: http://news
.bbc.co.uk/2/hi/4081999.stm (January 21, 2009).

11. Pink News, "Brazil congress rejects adoption by gay couples," available at: http://www.pinknews.co.uk/aroundtheworld/2008/08/brazil-congress
-rejects-adoption-by-gay-couples/ (January 17, 2009).

12. "Sexual Orientation and Legal Rights," available at: http://www.parl
.gc.ca/information/library/PRBpubs/921-e.htm (January 16, 2009).

13. University of Minnesota, Human Rights Library, "International Recognition of Same-Sex Relationships," available at: http://hrlibrary.ngo.ru/
edumat/hreduseries/TB3/act6/a6h3.htm (January 16, 2008).

14. "Spain votes in favour of gay marriage and adoption law," available at:
http://www.expatica.com/es/news/local_news/spain-votes-in-favour-of-gay
-marriage-and-adoption-law-21539_21368.html (January 20, 2009).

15. "Sweden legalises gay adoption," available at: http://news.bbc.co.uk/1/
hi/world/europe/2028938.stm (January 20, 2009).

16. Ibid.

17. "New Adoption Law Gives Gay Couples Joint Rights," available
at: http://www.ukgaynews.org.uk/Archive/2005dec/3001.htm (January 20,
2009).

18. Russian Gay Life, available at: http://gaylife.about.com/od/samesex-
marriage/ig/Gay-World-Tour.—_7/Gay-World-Tour—-Russia.htm (January 15,
2009).

19. http://www.letsgetequal.org.au/Info-legislative-recognition-same-sex
-relationshipsAU.doc (July 17, 2008).

20. Planetout.com, available at: http://www.planetout.com/news/article
.html?2007/08/02/2 (July 17, 2008).

21. Adoption Act 1988, available at: http://www.austlii.edu.au/au/legis/tas/
consol_act/aa1988107/s20.html (January 14, 2009).

22. "Catholics prepare for fight on gay adoption," available at: http://
www.smh.com.au/news/national/catholics-prepare-for-fight-on-gay-adoption/
2006/04/28/1146198353361.html (January 17, 2009).

23. "Same Sex Couples," available at: http://www.legalaid.qld.gov.au/Legal
+Information/Relationships+and+children/Relationships/Same+sex+couples
.htm (January 14, 2009).

24. Windy City Media Group, "South Africa OKs adoption," available
at: http://www.windycitymediagroup.com/gay/lesbian/news/ARTICLE
.php?AID=1187 (July 20, 2008).

25. "Attorney General rules same sex couples eligible to adopt," available
at: http://www.ynetnews.com/articles/0,7340,L-3505079,00.html (January 20,
2009).

26. "Christian Leaders in US Condemn Nigeria's Anti-Gay Bill," available
at: http://www.hrw.org/en/news/2007/02/26/christian-leaders-us-condemn
-nigeria-s-anti-gay-bill (January 14, 2009).

27. PinkNews, "March date for Sharia 'gay' trial in Nigeria," available
at: http://www.pinknews.co.uk/news/articles/2005-6878.html (January 15,
2009).

28. Adoption Law of the People's Republic of China, available at: http://www.china-ccaa.org/site%5Cinfocontent%5CZCFG_2005100901425793_en.htm (July 3, 2008).

29. Human Rights Watch, Europe: Gay Adoption Ruling Advances Family Equality," available at: http://www.hrw.org/en/news/2008/01/23/europe-gay-adoption-ruling-advances-family-equality (January 15, 2008); Children's Home Society & Family Services, India Adoption Requirements, available at: http://www.childrenshomeadopt.org/India_Adoption_Requirements.html (June 23, 2008); Queertry, available at: http://www.queerty.com/poland-rejects-eus-gay-adoption-ruling-20080123/; Partners Task Force for Gay & Lesbian Couples, available at: http://www.buddybuddy.com/immigr.html (June 10, 2008).

30. See "Adoption by Gays and Lesbians: A Survey of the Law in the 50 States and the District of Columbia," available at: http://www.adoptionpolicy.org/pdf/gaysandlesbian.pdf (January 14, 2009).

31. "Federal court orders Louisiana to recognize gay parents," available at: http://pageoneq.com/news/2008/Federal_court_orders_Louisiana_to_recognize_gay__1224.html (January 15, 2009).

32. "Florida Gay Adoption Ban Is Ruled Unconstitutional," available at: http://www.nytimes.com/2008/11/26/us/26florida.html (January 16, 2009).

33. "Arkansas Adoption Law," available at: http://www.hrc.org/your_community/953.htm (January 14, 2009).

34. "Arkansas: Adoption Law Is Challenged," available at: http://www.nytimes.com/2008/12/31/us/31brfs-ADOPTIONLAWI_BRF.html (January 14, 2009).

Conclusion

Summary and Concluding Comments

Before reporting on a country-by-country basis the rights and statuses of gay and lesbian communities, we summarized the legal status of gays and lesbians in the countries included in our study and reported on the countries not included in this study in which a death sentence is imposed on persons who are gay or lesbian. The latter include Afghanistan, Pakistan, Mauritania, Saudi Arabia, Sudan, and Yemen. We then reported the countries in which gays and lesbians were punished by life imprisonment. Those countries are Bangladesh, Bhutan, Guyana, Maldives, Nepal, Singapore, and Uganda. Table 1.2 in chapter 1 describes the penalties gays and lesbians receive in forty-two countries in which gay and lesbian behavior is illegal. The prison sentences range from twenty years to one year.

Of the countries included in our study Iran and Nigeria punish gay and lesbian behavior with a death sentence. In India, the maximum penalty is life imprisonment.

We then devoted four chapters to the attitudes of Christians, Jews, Muslims, Hindus and Buddhists toward homosexuality. None of the major religions endorse homosexuality but Christianity and Islam hold much more negative views than do Buddhism, Hinduism, and Judaism. And within Christianity, Catholicism holds more negative views than do most Protestant denominations. Within Judaism, Orthodox Jews and particularly Hasidic Jews view homosexuality as a grave sin.

In examining how gays and lesbians have been portrayed in films we concluded that Hollywood's most enduring stereotype of the gay man was that of a sissy. A less popular stereotype was that of the tragic homosexual desperately searching for love and happiness. The Children's Hour (1961) was the first major Hollywood film that depicted lesbianism.

Giovanni's Room by gay writer James Baldwin was one of the first American novels to deal with homosexuality.

Psychologists Havelock Ellis, Sigmund Freud, and Evelyn Hooker opposed criminalizing homosexual acts. Freud also held the view that homosexuality is nothing about which to be ashamed. It is not a vice, or a degradation, and it should be classified as an illness. Evelyn Hooker strongly opposed the view that homosexuals were psychiatrically disordered. Her studies led to the rescinding of homosexuality from the American Psychiatric Association Diagnostic and Statistical Manual of Psychiatric Disorders in 1973.

The Mattachine Society, founded in 1950 in Los Angeles, was one of the first gay movement organizations in the United States. The Mattachine Society called for gays to challenge anti-gay discrimination.

The Daughters of Bilitis (DOB) founded in San Francisco in 1950 was the first national lesbian organization in the United States. The group's activities included hosting a public forum on homosexuality, offering support to isolated and married lesbians, and participation in research activities.

Our country by country chapters showed that Nigeria, India, and Iran criminalize homosexuality. All of the other countries afforded gay and lesbian citizens varying degrees of legal recognition. The right of marriage is an especially contentious issue; currently only three of the countries we surveyed allow gays and lesbians to marry: Canada, Sweden, and South Africa. Other countries provide differing levels of rights; three countries nationally allow for registered partnerships: Germany, France, and Great Britain. While some countries do not provide for some rights on a federal or national level, certain countries have jurisdictions that provide these rights (e.g., certain states in the United States allow gays and lesbians to marry).

Several countries are struggling with the option of giving rights to gays and lesbians. In many countries like the United States, sentiment and treatment of gays and lesbians have evolved over the years. Although many countries are making advances in their laws in terms of providing equal rights compared to heterosexual citizens, gays and lesbians of every country still deal with some level of discrimination—if not from their governments, then from fellow citizens.

Eight countries provide immigration benefits for same-sex partners: Sweden, South Africa, Israel, Germany, Canada, Brazil, Australia, and Great Britain. Eleven countries allow gays and lesbians to serve openly in the military: Sweden, South Africa, Poland, Israel, Hungary, Germany, France, Canada, Australia, and Great Britain, and Argentina.

Responses to the public opinion surveys showed that public opinion on gay and lesbian issues varies from country to country, often corresponding to the country's policies and laws pertaining to gay and lesbian rights. We found the most accepting attitudes on homosexuality and gay and lesbian rights in France, Australia, Great Britain, Canada, Germany, Italy, and the United States. The most negative attitudes were reported in China, Egypt, India, Nigeria, Russia, and Poland.

Around the world, countries vary in the level of rights they provide to gay and lesbian couples in terms of adoption. Countries that allow adoption include Germany, Spain, Great Britain, South Africa, Israel, and Sweden. Countries that do not allow gays and lesbians to adopt include Italy, Argentina, Brazil, Hungary, Russia, Poland, India, and Iran. Other countries' laws are either vague, do not explicitly address same-sex parent adoption, or vary according to jurisdiction.

In this, the first published work on gay and lesbian communities the world over, we hope we have provided our readers with an in depth analyses of the status and the activities and beliefs of those communities.

Appendix

HOMOSEXUALS UNDER THE NAZI REGIME AND THE SOVIET UNION

No book on gay and lesbian communities and reactions to them would be complete without a discussion of their treatment under the Nazi regime and under Stalin.

Overall between 1933 and 1945 between 50,000 and 65,000 men were convicted for homosexuality. Thousands were tortured and killed in concentration camps. In 2003 the German government voted to erect a monument in Berlin for the homosexuals who were persecuted and murdered during the Nazi regime.

Homosexuals were identified by the pink triangles they wore on their prison uniform. Every prisoner had at least one of the following designations:

Jews:	A yellow triangle
Political prisoners:	A red triangle
Criminals:	A green triangle
Gypsies:	A brown triangle
Homosexuals:	A pink triangle
Antisocials:	A black triangle
Jehovah's Witnesses:	A purple triangle
Emigrants:	A blue triangle

Prisoners could have multiple designations: e.g., yellow and pink. The pink triangles were two or three centimeters larger than the others.

In 1928 the Nazi party expressed their views on homosexuality in the following statement:

> It is not necessary that you and I live, but it is necessary that the German people live. And it can only live if it maintains its masculinity. It can only maintain its masculinity if it exercises discipline . . . Free love and deviance are undisciplines. Therefore we reject you . . . Anyone who thinks of homosexual love is our enemy.

In 1929 the Reichstag Committee on the penal code recommended the abolition of paragraph 175 under which male homosexuality had been a criminal offense in Germany since 1871. But the reformed penal code was never acted upon before the Nazis gained power in January 1933, when Hitler was named Chancellor.

One month later, on February 23, 1933, homosexual rights organizations and pornography were banned. Three months later, on May 6, 1933, the Institute for Sexual Research was raided and destroyed. Collections of photographs and 12,000 books were confiscated and four days later at a mass public gathering in the center of Berlin they were burned.

By the summer of 1933 the Brown Shirts (SA) were raiding gay bars all over Germany.

1934 witnessed "The Night of the Long Knives." The occasion was the murder, ordered by Hitler, of one of his earliest supporters, Ernst Roehm, who was head of the S.A. Roehm was a homosexual. The leaders of the S.A. were all killed and hundreds of S.A. regulars were arrested and called "homosexual pigs." The S.A. was replaced by the S.S. under the leadership of Heinrich Himmler and his deputy Reinhard Heydrich. It was volunteers from among the S.S., called "Order of the Death's Head," who ran the earliest concentration camps beginning at Dachau in March 1933. During a six-week period in 1934, the Berlin police and the S.S. arrested more homosexuals than the Weimar Police had arrested in the 15 years of its prior rule.

On October 24, 1934, Himmler sent a secret circular letter to police headquarters throughout Germany instructing them to mail in lists of all "somehow homosexually active persons." On December 20, 1934, a Law Against Insidious Slander was issued to encourage relatives and neighbors to spy on one another. Information was generously rewarded.

On June 28, 1935, paragraph 175 was amended as follows:

175(a): A jail sentence of up to ten years or, if mitigating circumstances can be established, a jail sentence of no less than three years will be imposed on

1. Any male who by force or by threat of violence and danger to life and limb compels another man to indulge in criminally indecent activities, or allows himself to participate in such activities;
2. Any male who forces another male to indulge with him in criminally indecent activities by using the subordinate position of the other man, whether it be at work or elsewhere, or who allows himself to participate in such activities;
3. Any male who indulges professionally and for profit in criminally indecent activities with other males, or allows himself to be used for such activities or who offers himself for same.

As to how homosexuals were identified, the following are some of the ways:

In 1897 the central bureau of the Berlin criminal police had compiled lists of about 20 to 30 thousand homosexuals throughout the country. Added to this list were the names of those arrested after the Roehm purge, which included not only S.A. members but civilians found in gay bars. They were interrogated and forced to provide the names of friends and lovers. Bartenders were also pressured to produce names. Membership rosters and subscription lists of clubs, organizations, and magazines with a homosexual orientation were also seized. During the war the policy divided every city into administrative blocks. Each block was supervised by a block warden whose mission was to spy on everybody.

In 1937 the S.S. issued a chart that classified same sex felonies according to the following criteria:

1. Simple contemplation of desired object.
2. Plain touching (which might lead to hyperesthesia, erection, ejaculation, orgasm).
3. Petting, embracing, kissing by the partners with results similar to above.
4. Pressing of (naked) penis to any part of the partner's body, such as thigh, arm, hand, etc.

5. Pressing of two bodies against one another with or without friction.
6. Rhythmic thrusts between knees or thighs or in armpits.
7. Touching of penis by partner's tongue.
8. Placement of penis into partner's mouth.
9. Pederasty or sodomy (placement of penis in anus).

The Gestapo had no jurisdiction over the military, and thus it offered a relatively safe refuge for most homosexuals of military age. But in February 1942, as part of Hitler's purity decree issued in November 1941, originally directed at the S.S. and police officers, any male engaging in indecent behavior with another male, or allowing himself to be abused by him for indecent purposes, was to be condemned to death. As late as May 19, 1943, after the Russians had retaken Stalingrad and the German forces had surrendered in Africa, Himmler advised the army and many chiefs of staff that his bureau held jurisdiction over soldiers and sailors convicted of same sex indecencies.

Between 1940 and 1943 nearly 5,000 German military men were indicted for homosexual misdeeds. In the camps, homosexuals could sleep only in nightshirts and had to keep their hands outside the blankets. This was to prevent them from masturbating. The windows had several layers of ice on them. Anyone found in bed with his underclothes on, or his hands under the blankets—there were several checks every night—was taken outside and had several buckets of water poured over him before being left standing in the cold for a good hour. Only a few survived this treatment. The least result was bronchitis, and it was rare for any homosexual taken into the sick bay to come out alive. In other institutions, the gays shared quarters with Gypsies, asocials, or foreigners. Occasionally, homosexuals were distributed throughout various barracks and were treated no worse than other prisoners.

Plant offers five explanations for why most homosexual inmates were destroyed in the camps:

1. The homosexuals constituted one of the smaller minorities. Unlike antifascists, Jews, and foreign nationals who sometimes succeeded in setting up active inmate organizations, gays offered no challenge to the SS personnel.
2. The homosexuals were a decidedly heterogeneous group, and therefore hard to rally. Their members ranged from professionals and artists to hustlers and laborers. For political reasons some men had been stigmatized with a pink triangle, although

they had never committed crimes against Paragraph 175. In all, the gays offered the reverse pattern of those tightly bonded national groups who, in several places, fought for and gained minor food and work benefits.

3. Inside the camps, the barracks were run either by criminals or antifascists. Each of these factions, having once gained the power positions in the key offices, favored its own members in all vital areas of camp existence, especially food distribution, labor assignments, and sick-bay referrals. Thus, few Gypsies, homosexuals, clergymen, Jehovah's Witnesses, asocials, "race defilers," or armed forces deserters were placed in the privileged positions that offered some measure of relief from the daily trials. If an inmate could not slip into any of these jobs, his chances for getting out alive were extremely low. In addition, gays were often shipped to high-mortality tasks in factories and quarries.

4. Neither the hard-core criminals nor the antifascists were interested in cooperating with the homosexuals. To be sure, a green Kapo might pick an attractive young gay inmate as a favorite, but gays as a group did not profit from such an arrangement. The inmates themselves reflected the rejection that homosexuals had faced in Germany long before Himmler and Eicke had built penal colonies. On their side, the SS overseers were drilled to treat all prisoners as dangerous contragenics and to apply unremitting violence as the only appropriate method for keeping inmates under control. To them, homosexuals were despicable degenerates, and therefore they could and did indulge in manifold humiliation rituals.

5. Outside assistance was scant. Close relatives often would not lend support because they were ashamed that "one of the family" had been convicted for crimes against Paragraph 175. Former associates, friends, or lovers were even more reluctant—for good reasons. Thus the homosexual prisoners were virtually cut off from the world outside.

In the *Theory and Practice of Hell*, Eugene Kogan, who survived six years in Buchenwald where he was a political prisoner, described the situation of the homosexuals in the camps in the following terms:

The fate of the homosexuals in the concentration camps can only be described as ghastly. They were often segregated in special barracks and work details. Such segregation offered ample opportunity to unscrupulous elements in positions of power to engage in extortion and maltreatment. Until the fall of 1938 the homosexuals at Buchenwald were divided up among the barracks occupied by political prisoners, where they led a rather inconspicuous life. In October 1938, they were transferred to the penal company in a body and had to slave in the quarry. This consigned them to the lowest caste in camp during the most difficult years. In shipments to extermination camps, such as Nordhausen, Natzweiler and Gross-Rosen, they furnished the highest proportionate share, for the camp had an understandable tendency to slough off all elements considered least valuable or worthless. If anything could save them at all, it was to enter into sordid relationships within the camp, but this was as likely to endanger their lives as to save them. Theirs was an insoluble predicament and virtually all of them perished.

THE TREATMENT OF HOMOSEXUALS IN THE SOVIET UNION

After gaining power from the Czar, the Bolsheviks, in 1917, did away with all laws against homosexual acts.

The official Bolshevik attitude was that homosexuality did nobody any harm and that it was "if anything a scientific matter, not a legal one." They perceived the removal of laws against homosexual acts as an overall movement to extend sexual freedom, which was consistent with the goals of the revolution.

Soviet legislation declared an absolute non-interference of the state and society into sexual matters, so long as nobody is injured and no one's interests are encroached upon. But during the course of the 1920s there was a growing hostility on the part of the Soviet government and the press toward homosexuality. In the early phase of the anti-homosexual period, homosexuality was viewed as a sickness. Marriage and medical treatment could cure it. By the end of the decade there was a clampdown on gay authors and homosexuality was mentioned less and less in literary work; fiction, poetry, or theater. The clampdown on homosexual authors may have had as much to do with the authors' class backgrounds as with their homosexuality.

The growing hostility culminated in the passage of a new law, Article 154A of the Soviet penal code that was announced on December 17, 1933. The law outlawed sexual relations between men and prescribed five years of hard labor for voluntary sexual acts and eight years for acts involving the use of force or threats and for sex with a consenting minor. In January 1934 there were many arrests of homosexuals in Moscow, Leningrad, Kharkov, and Odessa. The arrestees included actors, musicians, and other artists. From 1930, homosexuality equaled opposition to the Soviet system.

Under Stalin (1929–1953) Soviet political police used homosexuals as informers and for recruiting foreign gay men for espionage. By the 1930s the Soviet press were involved in a campaign against homosexuality as a sign of "degenerality of the fascist bourgeoisie." Similar to events in Nazi Germany in the early and mid-1930s the repressive campaign against homosexuality did not occur in isolation, but went together with the abolition of legal abortion in 1936 and the exaltation of heterosexuality and the family as ideals for the Soviet citizen.

Yet, during the Stalinist age, Soviet persecution of gay men was neither continuous nor total. In the case of well-known personalities, such as Eisenstein, the popular opera tenor Sergei Lemeshev, the pianist Sviatoslav Richter, and numerous male ballet dancers, the authorities were willing to look the other way, provided the man was married and kept his homosexuality out of public view. A considerable number of Soviet gay men were in the Red army or the diplomatic corps or were entertainers. Most of them managed to escape detection and found ways to express their gay sexuality. According to Robert Conquest, leading historian of the Stalinist era, "It is very hard for the Western reader to envision the sufferings of the Soviet people as a whole during the 1930s . . . The "Great Terror" was launched cold-bloodedly at a helpless population. Everybody with unorthodox ideas was liable to end up in the camps: Jehovah Witnesses, Buddhists, Jewish Social Democratic Bundists, bourgeois nationalists, homosexuals, persons who had contact with foreigners." During the Stalinist era from 1929 to 1953, about 42 million people were killed.

Following Stalin's death, even though homosexuality remained a state crime, there were signs of change. Clandestine gay communities existed in the major cities. The works of gay and lesbian writers appeared in print. In 1973 a Textbook of Soviet Criminal Law was published in Leningrad that stated "no logical or scientific grounds had ever been stated in any Soviet juridical publication for criminalizing consensual sexual acts between males."

After the collapse of the Soviet Union in 1991, sodomy was decriminalized two years later and modern gay communities were visible in Moscow, St. Petersburg and other Russian cities.

Index

Page references followed by *t* indicate tables.

Page references followed by *t* indicate tables.

Page references followed by *t* indicate tables.

Page references followed by *t* indicate tables.

Page references followed by *t* indicate tables.

Page references followed by *t* indicate tables.

Orthodox Judaism, 13–14, 137

PACS. *See* Civil Solidarity Pact
Pakistan, 5, 137
Palestinians, 106
Pali Canon (Tripitaka), 23
Papua New Guinea, 4t
Paul, 8
pension and survivorship rights, 106, 106t
Pentecostal Protestants, 10
permanent partners, 59
Philip IV, 31
Plato, 25
Plutarch, 25–26
Poland, 97–99, 138–39; gay and lesbian adoption in, 131–32; legal status of gays and lesbians in, 3t; public opinion data, 98, 98t
premarital sex, 22
Presbyterian Church, 9
presidential candidates, 62t, 102, 102t
Pride Week (New York City, New York), 46
prison sentences, 5; death sentences, x, 5, 137; life imprisonment, 5, 137; in Nazi Germany, 143; penalties gays and lesbians receive, x, 3–5, 4t, 5, 137, 143, 146; same-sex felonies, 143–44; in Soviet Union, 146
Proposition 8, 57
Protestants, 10, 137
psychology, early, 39–41
public support: for adoption by same-sex couples, 60, 61t, 80, 80t; for gay and lesbian rights, 139; for same-sex marriage, 14–15, 60, 61t, 67, 68t, 72, 73t, 76–77, 76t, 80, 80t, 98, 98t, 102, 102t

Qatar, 4t

Queen Boat, 110
Qur'an, 17

Rebecca (1940), 35
Rebel without a Cause (1955), 35
Reconciling in Christ (RIC), 9
refugee status, 128
registered partnerships, 83, 93–94, 97, 138
religion: contempt of, 109–10. *See also specific religions*
Rhode Island, 57
Richter, Sviatoslav, 147
rights. *See* equal rights; gay rights; human rights
riots, 46
Robinson, Gene, 9
Roehm, Ernst, 142
Roman Catholic Church, 11, 29–30
Romans, ix, 8
Rome, ancient, ix
Rope (1948), 36
Rorshach inkblot test, 40
Russia, 101–3, 139; gay and lesbian adoption in, 131–33; public opinion data, 102, 102t. *See also* Soviet Union
Russian Federation, 3t
Russian Orthodox Church, 133

same-sex couples: in ancient Greece and Rome, 25–26; child adoption by, 131–36, 139; Christianity and, 8–9; civil unions, 9; death benefits, 58; equal rights for, 106, 106t, 127; legal recognition of, 51, 57, 67, 71–72, 73t, 75, 138; in Middle Ages, 30; pension and survivorship rights, 106, 106t; public support for, 14–15, 60, 61t, 72, 73t, 86–87, 86t; registered partnerships, 83, 93–94, 97, 138; religion and attitudes toward,

Page references followed by *t* indicate tables.

Page references followed by *t* indicate tables.

Page references followed by *t* indicate tables.

About the Authors

Rita J. Simon is university professor in the School of Public Affairs and the Washington College of Law at American University. She is the author or editor of more than sixty books.

Alison Brooks is a Ph.D. student in the Department of Justice, Law and Society at American University.